A POCKET GUIDE

THE
CUSTOMS AND
TRADITIONS
OF WALES

D0769708

A POCKET GUIDE

THE
CUSTOMS AND
TRADITIONS
OF WALES

TREFOR M. OWEN

CARDIFF
UNIVERSITY OF WALES PRESS
1991

© Trefor Owen, 1991

First published 1991
Reprinted 1993, 1995

British Library Cataloguing in Publication Data
A catalogue record for this book is available from the British
Library.

ISBN 0-7083-1118-0

The front cover shows the *Mari Lwyd* — a wassailing custom of
south Wales. During the Christmas season a man carrying a
horse's skull concealed under a white sheet and decorated by
ribbons was led from door to door.   (Photograph by kind
permission of the Welsh Folk Museum.)

Cover design by Design Principle
Typeset in Great Britain by BP Integraphics, Bath
Printed in Great Britain at The Bath Press, Avon

Contents

Acknowledgements

The author and publishers wish to thank the following copyright holders who have kindly permitted the reproduction of photographs.

Clwyd Record Office: St Winifred's Well (p. 79).

The London Borough of Bromley: Crystal Palace Challenge Trophy (p. 113).

National Library of Wales: Holyhead Wake (p. 91), cottage interior, Dolgellau (p. 31).

South Wales Miners' Library: handball court, Nelson (p. 69).

Welsh Folk Museum, St Fagans: peat cutting (p. 4), Melin Bompren (p. 8), *cist styffylog* (p. 10), *Ffair Dalis* (p. 12), *caseg fedi* (p. 13), *medel* (p. 14), hearth at Pontfaen (p. 27), stable loft (p. 34), puzzle jug (p. 39), *Mari Lwyd* (p. 44), wren house (p. 45), bidder (p. 57), *tŷ unnos* (p. 61), funeral procession, Trelech (p. 86), prayer meeting (p. 106), admission ticket (p. 109), Sunday school class (p. 110), trophy (p. 113).

Preface

The emphasis in this book is on the customs and traditions of Wales as they were to be found in the nineteenth century and after. True, most of these had their origins in the distant pre-industrial past and were sustained by a firmly established rural economy. Industrialization, however, was a renewing and transforming agent and not a mere destroyer of tradition. In the populous settlements which sprang up almost overnight on and around the coalfields, new forms evolved, taking the place of those seasonal customs which had proved ill suited to the harsh work regime of coal-mining and iron-working. Similarly, the religious upheaval following the Methodist Revival of the eighteenth century had equally far-reaching consequences for the popular culture of Wales. Ever critical of human frailties and the worldly diversions which pandered to them, the Nonconformists not only put down some of the more blatant manifestations of ungodliness, but also undermined many innocent pastimes. As a dominant force in a greatly expanded population, and with increasing self-confidence, they set about creating their own distinctive and respectable alternative culture epitomized by the choir, the eisteddfod and the literary meeting.

I have tried to deal in the various chapters with the major groups of customs and traditions based on the economy, the home, the community and the Church. I have sought to avoid covering the same ground as in my *Welsh Folk Customs* but a certain amount of overlap has been inevitable in dealing with some major customs. Lastly, our view of folk custom and tradition has been shaped by our methods of study and the historical sources available to us; these are treated in the final chapter, together with suggestions for further reading. To supplement the illustrations I have included contemporary descriptions, many of them by eye-witnesses, of customs which were not recorded by the artist and the photographer. Throughout the book I have used the old county names which disappeared from the administrative maps in 1974, but which are often more geographically precise and certainly more relevant historically than their successors.

I am indebted to Mr Arwyn Lloyd Hughes, Archivist of the Welsh Folk Museum, for his invaluable assistance in the selection of photographs, and to the National Library of Wales, the Clwyd Record Office and the South Wales Miners' Library for the use of material in their care. Finally, I am grateful to the staff of the University of Wales Press, especially Mrs Susan Jenkins and Ms Liz Powell, for their co-operation and help.

TREFOR M. OWEN
June 1991

1 Working the Land

The highlands and lowlands

Many Welsh customs are grounded in a farming tradition which has evolved over many centuries and which was governed by the opportunities offered by the physical environment. The existence of the central highland mass and its radiating valleys, which geographers have identified as a major factor affecting the preservation of so many features of Welsh life, also set limits to the way in which the land could be exploited agriculturally. More than a quarter of the surface of the country lies over one thousand feet above sea level, where the climate is correspondingly colder and wetter, and thus, with its shorter growing season, less conducive to arable farming, particularly the cultivation of wheat. Historically, the clearing of the valley bottoms and the coastal plains made possible the development of permanent settlements from the Dark Ages on. The economy of these lowland areas was based on a pattern of mixed farming which included both the growing of corn for human and animal consumption, as well as the keeping of cattle. The moorland zones, which were more thickly wooded in medieval times than at the present day, afforded summer grazing for the cattle during the growing season on the upland pastures, thus clearing the meadows for hay and releasing fields in the lowlands for the cultivation of cereals.

Seasonal migration and the 'hafod' economy

The system of migration or transhumance associated with the permanent settlement of the low-lying *hendre* and the *hafod* (pl. *hafodydd*) or upland summer pasture, with its seasonally occupied dwelling or *hafoty* (pl. *hafotai*), was an important feature of Welsh rural life, possibly from the Dark Ages until the end of the eighteenth century, or even later in some areas. It has left its mark on the landscape in the existence and layout of numerous hill farms, and on the place-names of the countryside.

Transhumance was practised in many parts of Europe as a means of exploiting the grazing which was available at higher altitudes during the brief period of summer growth. Only in the truly mountainous regions of the continent, however, was it practised on a dramatic scale involving the ascent of thousands of

1

feet to the temporary pastures and settlements. In Wales, with the partial exception of Snowdonia, both the distances and the altitudes involved were considerably less. It is thought that the summer grazing of the *hafodydd* on the extensive unenclosed waste lands of the settled townships of medieval Wales did not necessarily involve the construction of the temporary *hafotai* which appear to have been a later development. Nor were the summer pastures all on high ground; the badly-drained wetlands of low-lying Anglesey, for instance, were extensively grazed in this way. Nevertheless, as in Scotland and Ireland, transhumance played an important part in the traditional economy, with May Day (*Calan Mai*) and All Saints' Day (*Calan Gaeaf*), in all three countries, being the pivotal dates for the migration.

Life in the 'hafod'

This mountainous tract scarcely yields any corn. Its produce is cattle and sheep, which, during summer, keep very high in the mountains, followed by their owners, with their families, who reside in that season in *Hafodtai*, or summer dairy-houses as the farmers in the *Swiss alps* do in their *Sennes*. These houses consist of a long low-room, with a hole at one end to let out the smoke from the fire, which is made beneath. Their furniture is very simple: stones are the substitutes of stools; and the beds are of hay, ranged along the sides ... During summer, the men pass their time either in harvest work, or in tending their herds; the women in milking, or making butter and cheese. For their own use, they milk both ewes and goats, and make cheese of the milk, for their own consumption. ... Towards winter, they descend to their *Hên Dref*, or *old dwelling*, where they lead, during that season, a vacant life.

Thomas Pennant, *A Tour in Wales*, 2 vols. (1778–83), 2, 325–6.

In the classical description of the *hafod* economy in Wales given by Thomas Pennant who encountered it in Snowdonia in 1773, it will be noted that the seasonal migration involved tending cattle, sheep and goats, all of which were milked by the womenfolk. The cheese prepared from the milk of the ewes and goats was intended for immediate consumption, whereas the butter and cheese made from cows' milk, it is implied, was for later use on returning to the *hendre*. Evidence of a slightly later date from Llanfachreth, Merioneth, when a farmhouse was plundered while the family was at the *hafod*, would appear to confirm Pennant's statement that the entire family accompanied the animals to the high pastures, both men and women being engaged in their respective tasks of herding and milking in the vicinity of the 'summer dairies'.

The rise of sheep-farming and the decline of the 'hafod'

Pennant was writing at a time when the seasonal migration of human beings, if not of animals, was declining. Indeed, by the beginning of the nineteenth century the practice had virtually ceased. Its effect on the landscape and settlement pattern of the moorland districts, however, was long-lasting, as the temporary summer dwellings of the post-medieval period evolved into independent farms under the pressure of population growth and land scarcity. The *hafoty* at first probably consisted of a primitive cottage together with one or two small enclosures located on the edge of the summer pastures. Enclosure of the adjoining grazing seems frequently to have taken place during the sixteenth century and later, as contemporary disputes over ownership testify. A *hafod*, however, could become a viable independent farm only if it could grow enough fodder to feed its cattle during the winter months. The spread of sheep-farming in the late seventeenth and eighteenth centuries brought about a change in the *hafod* economy. Sheep did not require to be stall-fed—and part of the flock, if there was insufficient fodder, could be sent to 'winter' on farms in the coastal or other low-lying districts while the cattle in those districts were being stall-fed—a practice which has continued on a large scale and over long distances down to the present day. Whether the relationship was causal or not, the rise of sheep-farming on the mountain pastures coincided with the decline of the seasonal *hafod* and its replacement by a permanent farmstead usually bearing the same name. In central Wales the word *lluest* was commonly used for the simple shepherd's hut built on the sheep-walks and subsequently replaced by a small cottage, a process which Lewis Morris recorded in a survey of crown wastes and commons on the western slopes of the Plynlumon upland in north Cardiganshire in 1744. Many of these moorland settlements, whether *hafod* or *lluest*, remained occupied only as long as the pressure of the population on the land remained. Today

3

many are empty, except during the shearing season in June; others are ruins or have become summer homes, while the land is grazed by flocks from lowland farms.

Peat-cutting and the harvest of the moorlands

The tradition represented by the *hafod* is only one example of the exploitation of the extensive moorlands of Wales which, together with the mountains, even as late as the end of the eighteenth century, accounted for as much as two-fifths of the land area of the country. As deforestation took place in medieval times, and later, on the lower slopes and in the valleys, not only were the supplies of timber for building and for fuel depleted, but the peat deposits on the moorlands themselves were extensively worked for fuel. Peat-cutting traditionally began soon after *Calan Mai* (May Day), after the last frost on the exposed bogs and soon after the preparatory work on the cultivated land had been completed. Using the special paring irons and peat spades, the skilled work of trimming and cutting the peat bank was carried out, usually by a team of six or seven men. The drying of the cut peat, laid out and systematically turned over by the women and children, so as to ensure that the stiff breezes of the uplands could 'cure' the fuel, took place during late spring and early summer. At this juncture attention was temporarily diverted from peat-cutting to harvesting the bog-hay which was vital to the cattle-rearing of the low-lying farms of the moorland regions. Pennant's description, quoted above, refers to this activity in the *hafodydd* of Snowdonia, but on the lower undulating moorlands to the east the hiring of labour for the bog-hay harvest at midsummer, as at Llanuwchllyn in Merioneth, seems to have been more important in the local economy. In Ysbyty Ifan, Denbighshire, at the beginning of the last century, the farm of Cefn-garw was said to have two haystacks, each eighteen yards long, one of 'leafy hay' (*deil-wair*), and the other of bog-hay. The latter crop, however, despite its importance, was usually very sparse, and a man might carry on his back what had taken him a whole day to cut. After the bog-hay harvest, work on the peat was resumed, and the building of stacks of the now dry fuel took place on the moorland, at least some of it being subsequently transported to the peat shed in the farmyard.

Late summer, too, was the time to visit the moorlands to gather the rushes which would be made into candles during the winter evenings. In predominantly upland counties, such as Merioneth,

Cutting peat on the moorland above Llanuwchllyn, Merioneth.

similar forays would be undertaken over the summer months to collect lichen for use in colouring cloth; this was usually done by children who took with them their sacks and pieces of old scythes, with which to scrape the lichen from the rocks, usually collecting from six to twelve pounds in the course of a day. At the beginning of the last century a penny or two per pound was paid for the lichen gathered in this way, often at great danger to the children working on precipitous slopes. The upland areas also afforded an opportunity to harvest bracken for burning into ashes which were then taken to the coastal ports and exported to England for use in the making of soap. Oak and pitch-pine unearthed during peat-digging, were used as laths and lighting spills, respectively, and heather from the drier slopes was useful

Gathering lichen in Llanuwchllyn in 1816

I remember that our new house was a very poor new house. We were by then a large family, and a shilling a day, with his own food, was my father's wage during the winter half of the year, and half a peck of oatmeal cost us ten shillings and sixpence; so we could hardly obtain bread, not to mention relish, because of the expense. We were for a fortnight, once, without any bread, cheese, butter, meat or potatoes. ... The main thing we had to depend on was my father's wage; but, little by little, we children learned to knit stockings for sale, and in this way we earned a little. Eventually, my father and mother and the whole family were taken ill by a heavy sickness. We remained thus for a long time, and had to obtain parish assistance on that occasion. ... We all recovered gradually; my father took up his work once more, and we began to knit stockings, gather lichen, which we sold for a penny-ha'penny a pound, more or less, and thus helped our parents a little. There was hardly a stone of any size in all the mountains around our home that we did not know in the same way as we knew our neighbours, because we had been lichen-gathering so often in their midst. We had often been in peril of our lives as we climbed to search for the lichen; especially Margaret and I, on one occasion on a rock called Clogwyn-yr-eglwys in Pennantlliw-bach. Somehow we went to a place where we were for hours unable to get out of; but after we had been prisoners throughout the afternoon, we managed to come from there safe and sound in the evening, trembling above the frightening abyss.

W. Lliedi Williams, (ed.), *Hunangofiant ac Ysgrifau Ap Fychan*, 1948, 10–2. (Translated)

for a variety of purposes, including burning as fuel (especially for kindling fires and for baking), spreading as a dry base for hay stacks, and making serviceable brooms.

The wool-gatherers

As sheep-farming became more important during the eighteenth century and later, wool-gathering (or *gwlana*) was widely practised on the upland pastures, especially in central Wales. Parties of women from the coastal areas of Cardiganshire walked over twenty miles to the hill country between Tregaron and Llanwrtyd and combed the mountains and hedgerows for wool. Each party, consisting of about six women, brought sufficient food for a week or a fortnight, together with sacks for carrying the wool. Permission was sought to comb the land and to use barns or other buildings for accommodation, and the hospitality of the farmers was enjoyed in return for chores carried out around the farmyard. From two to four pounds of wool were gathered in the course of a day which started as early as four o'clock in the morning. A severe winter, followed by good growing weather in spring, led to shedding of more wool for the women to gather. Farther north, in parts of Denbighshire and Montgomeryshire, one or two fleeces would be set aside at shearing time for the wool-gatherers who visited the same farms every year and benefited from this sanctioned form of begging. The role of the moorland in the traditional economy and its 'culture of poverty' thus included far more than the seasonal grazing of the *hafod*.

The crops of the lowlands

Lower down the slopes of the central mass of mountains and moorlands with which we have been concerned in the last few pages, climatic and soil conditions are more favourable to cultivation and settlement. It is here, in the valleys radiating from the heartland and in the fertile coastal plains and plateaux which fringe it, that the agriculture of Wales has supported the bulk of the rural population for centuries. Even here, however, farming has been based more on a pastoral tradition, involving the rearing of cattle and sheep, than on arable farming to which the climate is not ideally suited. Nevertheless, although grass-growing for fodder has always been more important than the cultivation of cereals, there were many variations in farming patterns and in the emphasis placed on corn-growing. Far more importance was given to corn and roots for livestock-fattening in lowland Glamorgan and Gwent than in Gwynedd, which was a cattle-rearing area. The border counties of north Wales, on the other hand, devoted more attention to the production of butter and cheese, the central core of Wales, as we have seen, being sheep country. Despite the significance of animal husbandry, the cultivation of cereals was necessary for both human and animal consumption until the importing of foreign food and fodder began in Victorian times. Oats, and to a lesser extent barley, were grown more widely than wheat; nevertheless wheat cultivation was to be found in the more climatically favourable areas. A traveller in 1796 commented that 'along the north coast of Wales and up the Vale of Clwyd a great deal of fine wheat is grown; it seems the principal object of the farmer's attention'. Significantly, the same traveller adds that 'as you approach Wrexham the farmhouses improve and you begin to find them by outhouses as Barns, stables, etc. which is never seen on the West coast'.

Corn-drying kilns and the 'shimli' gatherings

The grain from the hardier crops more generally grown, particularly on the higher farms, often had to be ripened in the prolonged heat of the corn-drying kilns before it could be ground in the flour mills. From the eighteenth until the middle of the nineteenth century, which was the heyday of arable farming in Wales, corn-drying kilns were attached to many mills. Because of the warmth of the kiln floor which was heated from below during the drying process lasting up to forty-eight hours, the kilns were commonly

Melin Bompren mill and corn-drying kiln (on the right), Synod Inn, Cardiganshire, now re-erected in the Welsh Folk Museum, St Fagan's, Cardiff.

frequented by young people. The *shimli*, from the English 'assembly', as the informal meeting in the corn-drying kilns was called, became a popular institution, especially in Dyfed, where traditional tales were told and songs and ballads sung. Before the construction of the mill kilns, however, it was common to find primitive kilns built in the corner of a field, usually with a channel of several feet or yards to separate the grain from the fire providing the heat, so as to prevent a conflagration. The best fuel was thought to be straw from the corn which had provided the grain to be ripened. Fire was always a hazard in these field kilns and an early reminder of this is to be seen in a poem attributed (probably incorrectly) to the eminent fourteenth-century poet Dafydd ap Gwilym, namely 'Kywydd y crasu pan losgodd Dafydd ap Gwilym odyn i dad', which refers both to the occasion when the poet inadvertently burnt his father's kiln and to the *carthen*, or sheet of coarse woollen cloth, on which the grain was placed for heating. Field names including the word *odyn* (kiln) are a reminder (and an indication) of the former extent of this practice.

A diet of oats

Oats, not surprisingly in view of the climatic conditions, constituted a major element in the traditional diet of the people of Wales in one form or another. The great oatmeal chests (*cistiau styffylog*), which Pennant remarked upon when he visited the home of a Merioneth squire on his tour through Wales, 'held the essential part of the provision' and were important items of furniture in most houses of the period. A. R. Wallace, the scientist, described the everyday food of a farm in the Neath area of Glamorgan in 1841, including a supper dish of *sucan blawd* (steeped meal) 'formed from the husks of oatmeal, roughly sifted out, soaked in water till it becomes sour, then strained and boiled, when it forms a pale-brown sub-gelatinous mass, usually eaten with an abundance of new milk'. *Bwdram, picws mali, llymru, siot* and *brywes* were all variant forms of oatmeal dishes served with milk or buttermilk. A Merioneth witness giving evidence before the Royal Commission on Land at Bala, Merioneth, in the 1890s stated that the fare of the hill farmer, which had not changed very much since his childhood, consisted of bruised oatmeal cake and buttermilk in the morning, 'then we had some bread-and-butter and tea. For dinner we had bacon and potatoes. For tea, at about three or four o'clock, we used to have a lot of *sucan*, followed by a cup of tea...Then we had porridge or bread-and-cheese and

9

Of the 'rude' furniture which Thomas Pennant saw at Cwm Bychan, Merioneth, in the middle of the eighteenth century, the cistiau styffylog or oatmeal chests similar to the above 'held the essential part of the provision'.

butter milk for supper'. There were, of course, local variations in the diet, the border counties and the industrial areas apparently enjoying better fare, and Cardiganshire having as its staple dish *cawl*, or meat broth, which included mixed vegetables, some slices of salty home-cured bacon and bacon stock, often re-heated and served daily. Potatoes (and later rice) fitted in well with this *bwyd llwy* (spoon food) tradition in which fresh meat was of far less importance than dairy produce. Oats were also widely used to feed the horses which provided the motive power of Welsh farming in the nineteenth century, being mixed in some districts with crushed gorse cut on the marginal land of the farms.

Tenant farmers and smallholders
The corn harvest created a seasonal demand for extra help in the fields, and the way in which this problem was solved differed in various parts of the country. In Dyfed the cottagers and small-holders in the rural community traditionally helped at harvest time and in potato-lifting in return for the right to grow potatoes on the farmer's land and thus to provide for an essential part of their diet. The symbiotic relationship between the large tenant farmer and his neighbours in the 'little houses' extended to include such assistance as the services of a bull, the loan of a horse and cart and a supply of farmyard manure, as well as occasional small gifts of food and drink. It also pervaded community life, the farmer conveying in his wagons those families which helped him on the harvest field on a day's outing to the seaside in August on *Dydd Iau Mawr* (lit. 'Big Thursday'), as well as entertaining them to a meal on New Year's Day—a far more important occasion in this part of Wales than Christmas.

Hiring fairs
In contrast to this almost feudal relationship, the problem of seaso-nal labour in the harvest field of the corn-growing Vale of Clwyd in north Wales was solved by means of daily or weekly hiring fairs held in the villages and market towns. All the cottagers and labourers (some of whom had migrated temporarily from the sur-rounding moorlands to eke out their wages) assembled between four and six o'clock in the morning during the month-long harvest season if they were seeking employment that day, to be met by those farmers whose crops were ready to be harvested. Most farms sold a tub of butter before harvest time so as to have ready money to pay their labourers. The wage for the day was decided by the law of demand and supply and was recorded by a 'registrar' so that an objective calculation of the payments could be made when accounts were settled. The payment of 'Cross Wages' or *Cyflog y Groes*, so called because of the market crosses where the bargains were sealed, reflected a very different relationship between farmer and labourer from that which existed in Dyfed. We are told that the division between the two classes was much deeper, and was to be seen in the absence of a 'farming ladder' between them,

Ffair Dalis, *the well-known horse fair held at Lampeter, Cardiganshire, attracted buyers from all parts of the country.*

as well as in such features of social life as the lack of any intimacy in the home between the farmer's daughter and the maidservant, who was usually a cottager's daughter.

The corn harvest and the 'mare'

The harvest mare, or *caseg fedi*, was a well-known custom associated with the corn harvest, when it no doubt enlivened the back-breaking work of cutting and binding the sheaves. The term itself refers to the last tuft of corn which was subsequently made into an ornament. When the harvesting was nearly over, this last tuft was left standing and would be plaited and propped up so as to keep it upright. The reapers, who had been looking forward to this moment, would stand an equal distance from the 'mare'—generally fifteen to twenty yards—and prepare to throw their reaping hooks at it horizontally, just above the ground. If the sheaf had not been cut by the reapers in this way, it would fall to the lot of the head-servant to cut it, whereupon he (or the successful reaper) would shout

Bore y codais hi,
Hwyr y dilynais hi,
Mi ces hi, mi ces hi!

12

The caseg fedi *or corn maiden, made originally from the last tuft of corn to be reaped, developed into a decorative 'craft' souvenir.*

(Early in the morning I got on her track; late in the evening I followed her; I got her, I got her!)

He was then asked by the other reapers 'Beth gest ti?' (What did you get?), To which he, and the other reapers, replied 'Gwrach, gwrach, gwrach!' (A hag, a hag, a hag!)

In parts of Carmarthenshire the reply differed from this Pembrokeshire version, the last line being 'Pen medi bach mi ces!' (I got a little harvest mare), 'y gaseg ben fedi' (the end-of-the-reaping mare) being a local variation. Work having ceased, the rest of the day was given over to celebrating, an essential part of the proceedings being an attempt by the successful reaper to take the mare into the house without being found out by the womenfolk, who would be busy preparing the harvest feast. Bucketfuls of water would be thrown at suspected carriers in attempts to wet the mare (which would often be concealed in the clothing),

The medel *or reaping party on Y Fadfa farm, Talgarreg, Cardiganshire, in 1889.*

and success brought its reward in a limitless supply of beer and a place of honour at the table during the ensuing feast. If the bearer failed in his task, he forfeited his beer and was made a laughing stock and obliged to sit at the foot of the table. The mare itself was kept as a decoration in the farmhouse to prove that all the corn had been reaped. In a variant custom the 'mare' was sent to a neighbouring farmer who was behind with his harvest as a mild form of criticism. Ultimately, the 'mare' developed into the purely decorative 'corn dolly'.

As might be expected, there have been many attempts to explain the origin of this custom. The most likely is that the last tuft to be cut was thought to retain the potency of the entire crop and the power of vegetative growth and fertility which it contained. In one district, Llansilin, Denbighshire, corn from the dolly was mixed with the seed corn to be sown in spring 'to teach it to grow', as were the ashes from the yule-log. However, like the forms of neighbourly co-operation on the harvest field, which were discussed above, the custom did not survive the introduction of the self-binder in the late nineteenth century, which made it unnecessary to rely on *y fedel*, namely the reaping party consisting of neighbours and dependent cottagers.

Revelries of the hay harvest

The hay harvest, too, had its distinctive kind of conviviality which arose out of the co-operation in haymaking. As in the harvest mare custom, horse-play was involved, although in a less structured situation. Anybody entering a field in the Tenby district at haymaking time 'was immediately pounced upon by haymakers of the opposite sex, tossed about on the hay-cocks, and bound with hay bands, till a species of blackmail had been levied ... The ceremony when performed on females, was termed "giving them a green gown", and when on one of the other sex, "stretching their backs"'. In Brynaman, Carmarthenshire, the practice was referred to as *awr ar y gwair*, literally, 'an hour on the hay', and seems to have had the same sexual undertone.

The harvest meal

In contrast to the feast enjoyed after the corn harvest, the food during the hay harvest in many districts would be brought from the farmhouse and served out in the field, usually in a shady corner. Consisting mainly of *sucan* cooled until it had set into a kind of jelly which could be added to cold milk or beer, together with potatoes or bread and butter, neither this meal nor the afternoon tea could really compare with the corn-harvest feast. The emphasis in the course of the working day was naturally on quenching the thirst, and *siot*, in the form of oatcake crushed and steeped in buttermilk, was the popular drink for this purpose during haymaking. The supper served to the reapers after the corn harvest generally consisted of roast lamb and vegetables, together with a special dish, *whipod*, served as a pudding. This was a milk-based dish which included rice, eggs, flour and spice, boiled and then baked.

15

A Cardiganshire harvest feast
Penybryn, August 18, 1760. ... Here I am, with my little
harvest nearly all in. ... Tomorrow I am about to reap
rye, a sort of a feast day, such as the Hebrews made when
they sheared their sheep. I may have 40 or 50 neighbours
here to assist in reaping, and drinking of ale and eating
pasties and rams' fat. But for reaping all other corn we
pay dear enough, and this does not come very cheap, for
we must help those that help us. ... [August 20] Yesterday
there were 45 people reaping my rye, and some peas too—
breakfast of bread and cheese and milk and whey. Dinner
of *llymru* [flummery] and milk and bread and butter, but
the supper, namely the big meal, of a brewing-panful of
beef and mutton, and carrots and broth and wheat-flour
pudding, and about 20 gallons of light ale and more than
twenty gallons of beer, and putting the strings in the red
wooden fiddle, and a fiddler playing for them after they
had eaten their bellyfuls, and going to the barn on the wooden floor and dancing until they were sweating, a jug of
beer at their side, and a joy of tobacco for each one. What
a living!

J. H. Davies (ed.), *The Letters of Lewis, Richard, William and John
Morris of Anglesey, (Morrisiaid Môn), 1728–1765*, 1907–9, 2, 241–2.

As described in 1760 by one of the early recorders of folk culture,
Lewis Morris of Anglesey, the meal was washed down with plenti-
ful supplies of drink and the evening rounded off with dancing
to the music of the fiddle.

Ffest y pen (the end-of-harvest feast) was known in Llanfyllin,
Montgomeryshire, as *cwrw cyfeddach* (carousal beer) and in Caernarfonshire as *bodddi'r cynhaeaf* (drowning the harvest), both of
which indicate the traditional nature of the celebration of this
critical turning point in the farming calendar. In the late nineteenth
century, when *y fedel* became less important after the spread of
the self-binder, the evening meal served on the threshing day (following the introduction of the steam-driven thresher which gave
rise to the need for a new occasion for neighbourly co-operation)
tended to rival the harvest supper in importance.

16

One of the other important farming occasions, especially in the upland districts, namely sheep-shearing day, likewise involved the preparation of elaborate meals for the co-operative work team, a dinner of cold beef, potatoes and peas, followed by rice pudding, being the usual fare, with a plain tea in the afternoon. On all these occasions the family concerned not only wished to acknowledge the help it had received but also to maintain its reputation for hospitality.

The shepherds' feast and other customs
A somewhat different kind of celebration associated with sheep-farming was *ffest y bugeiliaid* (the shepherds' feast) or *ffest Awst* (the August feast). This took place on 12 August when all the shepherds in a particular area—often lads between ten and thirteen years old who were employed between April and October to herd both sheep and cattle—would bring their own food to hold a feast on a hilltop or bank. This would be followed by racing and jumping and similar feats until nightfall. This custom (recorded in Llandysul, Cardiganshire) is reminiscent of the tradition in various districts in south Breconshire of ascending the Brecon Beacons on horseback between dinner and supper on the first Sunday in August. A fatal accident, which took place about 1850, when two youths fought over a girl and fell to their deaths, put an end to the practice. A similar custom observed on the same day in the upper Swansea valley, when young people visited Llyn y Fan, was transformed into a preaching festival in the mid-1800s. Hilltop and mountain gatherings celebrating Lammastide on the first day (or Sunday) in August are an old tradition which has its counterpart in the Lughnasa festival in Ireland where seventy-eight examples have been recorded.

Co-operation, thrift and barter
The various forms of co-operation and the accompanying conviviality which have been discussed above were grounded in an economy which involved the exploitation of the natural environment to the utmost so as to avoid all unnecessary expenditure. Money was scarce, and, as an eighteenth-century traveller commented, 'frugality has charms in Wales where the knowledge of the old adage is perfectly understood that "saving is getting".' The rural economy of the Welsh countryside was, of course, never entirely self-sufficient, and the produce of the land had to be sold to meet the obligatory expenditure on rents, tithes, taxes and wages. The

17

cattle drovers, driving their beasts eastward over the moorlands to be fattened on the lush lowland pastures of England and eventually sold in Barnet fair, Hertfordshire, were an essential link between producer and market and the agents of new fashions and ideas; other markets, principally in poultry and dairy produce, were more locally organized. Alongside this production for sale, however, there was a strong subsistence element based on what the farmer could produce himself and on the careful husbanding of natural resources so as to avoid having to spend the money earned. We are told of Dinas Mawddwy, Merioneth, in the last century, for example, that 'according to the old people there were three ways which led to the workhouse, namely buying peat, buying bread and buying fresh meat'. Thrift, in fact, meant not only doing without certain things it was possible to buy, but also making the most of what you had and what you could get. By various stratagems the potentially disruptive influence of the market could be kept at bay. One way in which this was attempted was by relating items of expenditure on the farm to the expected income. The annual rent of a farm, for example, might be calculated on the basis of the number of animals it could produce each year. In the Builth district of Breconshire, we are told in 1893,

> Farm rents are calculated on the basis of £10 for every cow on a stock-rearing farm, and farms are spoken of as 5-cow farms or 10-cow farms, as the case may be. This was the old plan; the cows paid the rent by the value of their calves, and all the rest belonged to the man to pay for rates and taxes, and profit. A fall in the price of heifers upsets the calculation, but cows must continue to be kept, if only for the purpose of consuming the long grass which the sheep will not eat.

The last sentence, incidentally, indicates how inflexible the regime could be as a result of important ecological considerations. Another tradition reflecting the urge to curb the influence of the market, this time in the Llŷn peninsula, was that the annual wage of the *hwsmon* or head servant should ideally correspond to the price obtained for a bullock. A better way still, from this standpoint, was to avoid monetary payments entirely, if at all possible. Labourers were often paid in kind, one sheaf in ten (or more), for example, being given to the labourer engaged to thresh the corn with a flail during the winter months. The right to graze a sheep or two on the farmer's field was sometimes part of the bargain struck when employing a manservant; and by means of

the custom known in Dyfed as *llafur golym* a farmer might give
the blacksmith a stack of corn each year in payment for the shar-
pening of various farm tools. As in other countries, too, the miller
was remunerated in kind for grinding the farmer's corn, his 'toll'
being exacted before the flour was returned to the customer. The
amount of money circulating in the countryside, through these
devices, might be kept quite low, as surviving farm account books
(where any were kept), suggest; but transactions relying on barter
and payment mediated through these customs were correspondingly greater in number and permeated the social life of country
people.

Smallholders and the 'scavenging economy'

Subsistence activities, engaged in for similar reasons, whilst
obviously limiting the amount of money spent, entailed the expenditure of other resources, notably labour and time, which were
often more readily available. Such activities were most numerous
in what has aptly been termed the 'scavenging economy' of the
smallholder or cottager. A glimpse of what this entailed in the
beginning of the nineteenth century is afforded in the following
contemporary account based on the life of an Anglesey peasant:

> Little money was circulated. It was necessary to live thriftily,
> for the price paid for a fat pig was only 1½*d.* a pound, and
> no more than about £5 could be got for a fat cow. They cut
> turves and peat for their fuel, pulled up rushes from the root
> and peeled them to make rush candles to illuminate the long
> winter nights. Thus, between everything, no more than 5*s.*
> would be spent in a year on heating and lighting. Little was
> spent on food, for they lived entirely on the produce of the
> land.

A similar impression is left by a description given by the antiquary
William Williams (1738–1817) of the domestic economy of an agricultural labourer in Llangristiolus, Anglesey, in the middle of the
previous century. The husband found employment threshing in
winter, and his share of the corn kept him in bread for the whole
year as well as feeding his pig. His winter evenings were spent
peeling and combing the hemp grown in his garden for his wife
to spin, as well as making clogs and baskets. His wife spun not
only hemp but also wool earned from the medicines she had prepared for neighbouring farmers, using herbs grown in their half-
acre garden. The garden also supplied them with potatoes, beans,

carrots and onions, which formed their staple diet, together with bacon from the pig and eggs from the two ducks and a drake, and the two hens and cockerel which she kept, as well as a corgi and a cat. For her herbal remedies she also received milk and butter which, with beans, peas, carrots and eggs, comprised their summer diet. Their winter fare consisted of potatoes and turnips, potato broth peppered with an onion in it, pea broth flavoured with a slice of bacon. Their garden also contained five or six apple trees and some gooseberry bushes. The wife also knitted stockings—a common way of supplementing income in the moorland districts also—and sewed throughout the year, as well as washing and baking, cleaning the cabin and feeding the pig. The pig, indeed, in many communities was an indicator of subsistence; being a scavenger, it ate unpalatable food, but could in its turn be eaten, or, as often happened, sold to pay the rent. It was a significant element in the economy of the smallholder throughout Wales. The Revd Walter Davies, 'Gwallter Mechain', the agricultural writer, in his diary for 1813, commented in Ystrad Meurig on the importance of pigs in upper Cardiganshire, thousands being exported every year. His hurried entry reads, 'Quick return of money—one year—must wait 3 for the growth of an ox. Store pigs reared cheaply—on whey—refuse of potatoes etc—a couple of pigs selling from £10 to 15 or 20 is a consid. assistance for a small farmer to pay his rent'.

Free pickings from land and sea

Wild plants could be gathered for human consumption too, notably mushrooms, blackberries, nuts and watercress. This form of activity, together with the collecting of plovers' eggs, was regarded by Anglesey farmers as depredation and a nuisance in their evidence to the Royal Commission on Land in 1894. In many areas, especially those fringing the moorlands, the making of birch wine from sap drained from the tree was another ingenious use of natural resources. 'Berry cider' was made in the Cadair Idris district in Merioneth from the berries of the mountain ash gathered by the poor; boiling water was poured on to the berries and in a month or so resulted in a pleasant acid drink. On the coast, collecting shellfish was a common means of eking out the food supply, both directly for human consumption and indirectly through the keeping of ducks fed on mussels. Fuel, too, could be supplemented in treeless districts such as the Llŷn peninsula by scavenging the fields to collect cow dung for drying and using

Pig-keeping and saving money

But this is what I say—and I'll say it to my dying day—that for a poor man—a man paid by his working day—that he can do no better than keep a pig, especially if there are some wild carrots and nettles growing near his house—champion food for a pig. This is how I see things—keeping a pig is exceedingly like the savings bank. You'd never say, strictly speaking, that the savings bank pays—for man alive what is two-and-a-half? It's not worth a man putting what little money he has there—that is, for the sake of the interest. And yet no man in his senses would deny that it is a good thing to put money in the savings bank. To my mind,—and, for an ordinary man, I have bred as many pigs as anyone in the country—keeping a pig pays much better than the savings bank. This is why: think of a man who decides to live frugally and to put his money in the savings bank. Very good. Say that he saves a shilling a week. Right. But some weeks it will be tight on him—he will have lost a day's work—or he will be tempted to buy something he doesn't want, and the savings bank can take its chance, and by the end of the year there'll be ever so little in the bank. But if the man had a pig and a conscience to feed it well, he'd be bound to find food for it even though he'd have to go short himself. And I'll tell you another thing—a man doesn't like taking mere trifles to the bank, and if he tries to keep them in the house until they grow into a big enough sum, some misfortune is always going to take them away.

From the novel by Daniel Owen, *Profedigaethau Enoc Huws*, 1891, 108. (Translated)

to give a swift but short-lived heat on the hearth. In parts of the country, such as Breconshire, where a moderate tree cover still remained, especially in the hedgerows, the poor were allowed to collect the broken twigs left over in May, after the farmer had taken what he needed for his own use, restricting himself to what he could lift on his pitchfork, so as to leave some for the poor. Arrangements of this sort, while not always acceptable, especially when trespass and poaching were involved, but usually based on a mutual understanding, were built into the very fabric of social life in the countryside. In their extreme form they constituted a sanctioned means of begging, tolerated only because of the dire poverty of the times.

The folklore calendar

It is not surprising in view of this intensive exploitation of the land to find that there were traditional guidelines to farming practice which were embedded in folklore. These beliefs recommended the correct time to carry out certain operations. For example, in the Builth district of Breconshire the time to turn the barren

Making and using rush candles in Breconshire

Until about the middle of the last century many rush candles were burned in our country, especially by families in comparatively low circumstances. The best time of the year to cut rushes for candles was when the harvest moon was full. If they were cut earlier in the summer, the wick would not have filled and ripened in the rush; and if the rushes were left until later before being cut, the peel would have thickened and have become more difficult to peel. People often went afar to cut rushes for candles in order to get good ones, and they were bound in large sheaves to be carried home. After they had had a little time to wither and dry, they were cut to the appropriate length. About a foot, or a little more, was the the length of the rush candle. During the hours of leisure, some members of the family would come together to *pabwyra* (peel rushes), and while they were engaged in that work they would sing the old tune *Hyd y frwynen* [lit. 'the length of the rush']. After peeling the required quantity, the rushes were bound in small bunches to be set aside until a suitable time; and the necessary number would be dipped in molten wax and placed on a slate to solidify, after which they could be burned as required. The rush candle would last about twenty minutes (or a little longer). Before clocks were common, many families used to calculate when it was time to go to bed in winter by the number of candles burned.

Cymru, 67 (1924), 147–8 (Translated)

cattle out in spring was when the first flower of the *penllwyd* (cud-weed) was seen on the moorland. In the northern counties the corresponding plant was *y filfyw* or figwort. Peat-cutting began after the last spring frost, which might damage the turves as they lay in the bog, and after the sap, which peat was thought to contain, had risen to improve its combustible quality. The best time to cut rushes for making rush-candles was when the harvest moon was full. If they were cut earlier, the rush stem would not have filled out and ripened; if left too late, the peel would have thickened and would be harder to remove. Autumn was the time to cut and plait withies for use in basket-making, before the sap had disappeared entirely from the wood, or in spring when the vigour of that season was beginning to rise in it. Frequently the advice was contained in the form of a verse which could be easily memorized, as in this Breconshire example:

Pan fo'r ddafad yn mynd i hwrdd
Mae cymryd ffwrdd y dderwen,
A phan fo'r ddafad yn dod ag o'n
Mae mynd at fôn yr onnen.

(When the sheep is taken to the ram is the time to take away the oak; and when the sheep brings forth its lamb is the time to cut the ash.)

Farming operations were also governed by the church calendar and integrated with the feast days, as was common throughout Christendom. Important occasions in the farming year were linked to traditional festivals, some of which were undoubtedly pre-Christian in origin; for example, sheep-shearing took place on St John's Day (*Gŵyl Ifan*) celebrated at midsummer. On other, less important, feast days, such as St Mark's Day (25 April), work was prohibited, but like many of the farming traditions discussed in this chapter, such prescriptions and restrictions have long since fallen into abeyance.

2 Customs of Hearth and Home

The meaning and symbolism of the 'aelwyd'

In the previous chapter we saw how the land and its working gave rise to traditions and customs which remained a feature of Welsh life for many centuries. We now turn to those elements which centred on the house and hearth. In a society having a dispersed rural settlement pattern, for the most part, and displaying strong centrifugal tendencies, domestic life and the peripatetic customs associated with it undoubtedly occupied an important place.

The Welsh word *aelwyd* has a wider connotation than 'hearth'. It is almost synonymous with 'home' and even 'family'; indeed the meanings of the word are given in the University of Wales Dictionary as, first, 'home', 'dwelling'; secondly, 'stock','kin'; and thirdly, 'fire', 'fireplace', 'hearth'. Traditionally in Wales the hearth was in both a symbolical and a literal sense the focus of a home—the Latin *focus* meaning 'fireplace'—and the converging point of family activities from time immemorial, and as such, it has always occupied a prominent place in Welsh folklore. In many farmhouses, nineteenth-century writers tell us, the fire was reputed to have been kept burning continuously for centuries; to let it go out was to invite bad luck. The tasks of *enhuddo* (covering) and *dadenhuddo* (uncovering) the fire every evening and morning were taken very seriously in Wales and in the other Celtic countries. In the Hebrides, for example, an elaborate ceremony was performed nightly in which the names of the God of Light, the God of Peace and the God of Grace were solemnly invoked as three peats were laid down on the hearth before being covered with ashes to the accompaniment of an intoned formula. In Wales the 'seed of the fire'—a glowing ember of peat or wood—was singled out and replaced on the hearth after it had been swept clean. It was then covered with ashes for the night, to become by the following morning the nucleus of the new day's fire. When the fire in a new house was lit for the first time it would be kindled with embers taken from the fire in the old house—a reflection of the importance of the fire on the hearth as a symbol of the continuity of family life. The word *dadanudd*, deriving from the daily process of uncovering the ashes to allow the fire to burn

A medieval domestic interior

And as they came towards the house, they could see a black old hall with a straight gable end, and smoke a-plenty from it. And when they came inside, they could see a floor full of holes and uneven. Where there was a bump upon it, it was with difficulty a man might stand thereon, so exceedingly slippery was the floor with the cows' urine and their dung. Where there was a hole, a man would go over the ankle, what with the mixture of water and cow-dung; and branches of holly a-plenty on the floor after the cattle had eaten off their tips. And when they came to the main floor of the house they could see bare dusty dais boards, and a crone feeding a fire on the one dais, and when cold came upon her she would throw a lapful of husks on to the fire, so that it was not easy for any man alive to endure the smoke entering his nostrils. And on the other dais they could see a yellow ox skin. And good luck it would be for the one of them whose lot it would be to go on that skin ... And the woman lit a fire of sticks for them and went to cook, and brought them their food, barley-bread and cheese and watered milk ... And when their resting-place was examined there was nothing on it save dusty flea-ridden straw-ends, and branch butts a-plenty throughout it, after the oxen had eaten all the straw that was on it above their heads and below their feet. A greyish-red, threadbare, flea-infested blanket was spread thereon. and over the blanket a coarse broken sheet, in tatters, and a half-empty pillow and a filthy pillow-case thereon, on top of the sheet. And they went to sleep.

The house of Heilyn Goch as described in 'The Dream of Rhonabwy' *c.* 1300–25. Gwyn Jones and Thomas Jones (translators), *The Mabinogion*, 1949, 137–8.

afresh, had a figurative meaning in the Welsh Laws which, although codified in the twelfth century, incorporated much earlier material. When a man claimed land belonging to his ancestors from which he had been dispossessed, he could assert his legal right by lighting a fire on the old hearth.

The association between the fire on the hearth and legal ownership of the house persisted for hundreds of years, for, as late as the nineteenth century, as we shall see, the *tŷ unnos* or squatter's cottage built hastily overnight was not complete—and the right to ownership not secured—according to popular tradition, until the fire had been lit and smoke came through the chimney the following morning. According to the medieval Welsh Laws, too, the *pentanfaen* or fireback stone, once it had been placed in position on the hearth, might not be removed even though the house were deserted: it stood 'as a perpetual sign that the site was once that of an occupied homestead'. These pervasive and persistent associations are probably sacred and pre-Christian in origin, as indeed archaeological evidence suggests: even before houses were built, fire was central to man's life.

Cooking on the open hearth

In the earliest known houses, dating from prehistoric times, the fire burned on an open hearth in the middle of the floor or against a gable wall, the smoke finding its way out through a hole in the roof. Archaeological finds from this early period include cauldrons belonging to the middle of the first millenium BC which were found in the Llynfawr deposit in Glamorgan and probably used for boiling meat and vegetables, as were similar utensils until recent times. Bakestones or griddles, which are mentioned in the Welsh Laws, complemented this form of cooking and likewise remained a prominent feature of the traditional kitchen for many centuries, together with the tripod used on the open hearth in conjunction with the griddle and inverted baking pot. The vertical fireback stone and the horizontal hearthstone placed in front of it, on which the fire permanently rested, could be supplemented, when required, so that an open hearth could accommodate a large number of cooking vessels. An eighteenth-century traveller commented on this convenient arrangement which he saw during the preparations for a wedding feast in Cwm-y-glo, near Llanberis, Caernarfonshire:

A fire of square peat and sufficiently dried,
Was spread on the hearth, and at least four feet wide;
Over which took their stations six kettles or more,
Which promised a feast, when they opened their store;
And round this flat furnace, to keep them quite hot,
Were plac'd twelve more vessels, which held—God knows
    what,

> Four cooks in short bed-gowns, attend by desire,
> Like the witches in Macbeth, to stir up the fire.

Another traveller, at the beginning of the nineteenth century, visiting a 'most miserable dwelling' in upland Merioneth, noted the size of its open hearth: 'in the centre [of the single room], about two yards square was a fire of turf on the ground'. Cooking arrangements were flexible on hearths of this size; in addition a baking pot and tripod could be taken out of doors or to an outhouse to be used if this was more convenient.

The fire on the floor at Pontfaen, Ciliau Aeron, Cardiganshire. The adjustable crane and iron pots, bellows and tongs, settle and armchair (on either side of the open hearth) were among its traditional elements.

Architectural developments of the sixteenth century

The 'hall house' of the Middle Ages retained the open hearth in the large central room which was usually open to the roof and flanked by one or two smaller rooms. It was the coming of the chimney and the introduction of a first floor, two developments which often occurred at the same time, which resulted in the flowering of vernacular architecture in the sixteenth century and later, reflecting the trend towards increased comfort and privacy. The regional types of house plans dating from this period arose from the various ways in which these new architectural elements, and other features, such as the staircase, were incorporated in the structure of the buildings. Henceforth, the hearth had to be located against a wall and to have a chimney to convey the smoke past the upper floor; but it remained an open fire and the focus of domestic life. In wealthier households highly decorative cast-iron firebacks, often bearing heraldic arms, served both to protect the wall behind the fire and, no doubt, to throw out some of its heat to the room. Hobs were built on both sides of the fire to keep it in place and to hold some of the cooking utensils; and the introduction of a pit, covered by an iron grid, allowed the ashes to be removed easily and the fire to be adequately ventilated. The pit, appropriately called *uffern* (hell), with its constant warmth, was used to rear weak chickens, hence the saying 'Cyw a fegir yn uffern, yn uffern y myn fod' (A chick reared in hell will want to stay in hell).

The customs of wood-burning

The fuel burnt on the open hearth had been wood or, as supplies dwindled with the continuing deforestation over the centuries, peat. Local traditions recorded in the last century in Breconshire gave the countryman advice on which wood to burn at different times of the year. As often happens, the advice was expressed in the form of a verse which could be easily remembered:

Gwern a helyg hyd Nadolig,
Bedw os cair hyd Gŵyl Fair,
Cringoed y caeau o hyn hyd Gla'mai,
Briwydd y fran o hynny ymla'n.

(Alder and willow until Christmas, birch, if available, until Candlemas, withered branches from the fields from then until May Day, the small twigs of the crow from then on).

Other sayings expressed the superiority of the wood of certain trees, for example, 'onnen o'r ffos, a derw o'r daflod' (ash from the ditch, oak from the cockloft), that is, even a wet ash tree burns as well as dried oak.

The yule-log

During the Christmas season, when prolonged warmth was needed for the celebrations which continued over several days, the yule-log was burned. It was usually placed 'at the back of a large square hearth, the fire for general use being made up in front of it, the embers raked up to it every night, and the log carefully tended that it did not go out. During the twelve days of Christmas no light must be struck, given or borrowed'. Although this description relates to Eastridge Coppice in Shropshire, the *cyff Nadolig*, as it was called in Welsh, was also to be found in Wales. A brief reference to the practice in Penmachno, Caernarfonshire, confirms that the log was placed behind the fire, and in the border district of Llansanffraid-ym-Mechain, Montgomeryshire, ashes preserved from the yule-log were thought to be 'infallible in preventing evil, and a portion was carefully kept for the next "seedness", and was placed in the first hopper with the seed corn to act as a charm, and thus cause the corn to grow and become a fruitful crop'. The burning of the yule-log was a practice of considerable antiquity in Wales and is referred to in the poetry of Guto'r Glyn (*c*.1435–*c*.1493) and Tudur Aled (*c*.1465–*c*.1525).

Coal, peat, gorse and other fuels

Coal, which appears to have been introduced into the wealthier homes in medieval times, was decidedly a luxury with its own requirements for efficient burning. George Owen, the Pembrokeshire historian and topographer, complained in 1603 of the increasing shortage of wood in the county, and stated that coal was widely used, most of the gentry who were 'well served with wood' preferring it as a fuel if it could be brought easily by water to their homes. His evidence suggests that coal was less widely used for heating the living rooms than for cooking food. Coal was 'voyd of smoake where yll chimnies are', gave a 'readie fier' and was 'very good and sweete to rost and boil meate'. Furthermore, it 'doth not require a mans labour to Cleave wood & fed the fier contynuallie', and was generally to be preferred to wood for its smell. Pembrokeshire 'stone coal', once kindled, 'geaveth a greater heate than light, and deliteth to burne in darke places' and 'is burned in Chimneies and grates of Iron'. Peat was little inferior to coal except when 'yll seasoned', that is, improperly harvested, or 'yll placed to burne in the house, as out of Chymneies' when the smell was loathsome. Gorse, which was extensively used for baking and brewing, often grew so large that it was suitable as a principal fuel in halls, chambers and kitchens, giving a 'sweete' fire, clearer than that of any other wood, and yielding greater heat. Fern was the fuel of the poor, and heather was the 'sweetest fuell for drieing of Mault'.

Owen's evidence is interesting not only because it assesses the relative usefulness and suitability of the various fuels which were available in the Pembrokeshire countryside, but also because it reflects the introduction of the grate and the chimney in association with coal burning. The free-standing early grates merely raised the fire above the level of the floor so as to allow a draught to reach the burning coal; by means of an iron bar grating they also kept the fire in its place and allowed the ash to fall. The burning of culm, a mixture of coal dust and clay formed into balls, is not mentioned by George Owen, despite its subsequent popularity in Pembrokeshire; probably its spread was related to the more extensive use of grates for which it was best suited.

Ovens

Attention was given to specialized functions, too, and the introduction of bread ovens, generally dome-shaped and made of a coarse clay earthenware, represents another innovation on the hearth, especially in south-east Wales where ovens imported from Bideford in north Devon are to be found from the seventeenth century on. Elsewhere in Wales the built-in stone or brick oven, usually placed alongside the fireplace, is more common. This was heated separately from the fire, either using gorse kindling or ashes taken from the fire, which were subsequently removed before the oven was used. Its opening was covered with a stone slab and sealed around the edges with clay so as to retain enough heat to bake the bread. During the nineteenth century, following the introduction of rice, it became usual to place a rice pudding in the oven when the bread was taken out, an interesting example of the integration of a new food into an old tradition. The earlier tradition of baking bread in a baking pot covered with burning peat on the open hearth or out of doors survived in many parts of Wales until the present century. Separate outside bakehouses were also to be found, as were baking ovens in back kitchens. In these locations brewing, laundering and the preparation of food for the animals, were carried on alongside baking. The traditional monopoly of the hearth, with its portable equipment which could also be used out of doors if required, thus frequently gave way to other arrangements for carrying out these domestic processes. In the house itself, the kitchen range, combining hobs, baking oven and boiler with a central coal-burning fire, often replaced the large open fireplaces of earlier times when the use of coal spread in the nineteenth century. In both industrial and rural areas, however, the range maintained the primacy of the kitchen as the main living room where work, food and leisure were combined.

The single hearth
Until recent times most houses had but one heated room, and many had only a single room. From the returns of the Hearth Tax levied in the seventeenth century it is possible to estimate how prevalent the single-hearth house was in some parts of Wales. In the parish of Llanuwchllyn, Merioneth, for example, it was

Cottage interior at Dolgellau, Merioneth, c. 1836, by Edward Pryce Owen. This depicts the daubed wickerwork hood over the fireplace and the utilitarian contents of the period.

Cottages in mid nineteenth-century Merioneth

I visited many cottages in Tal-y-llyn and the adjoining parish of Llanfihangel. The house accommodation is wretched. The cottages are formed of a few loose fragments of rock and shale, piled together without mortar or whitewash. The floors are of earth; the roofs are wattled, and many of these hovels have no window. They comprise but one room, in which all the family sleep. This is in some cases separated from the rest of the hut by wisps of straw, forming an imperfect screen. These squalid huts appear to be the deliberate choice of the people, who are not more poor than the peasantry in England. They are well supplied with food, clothing and fuel; every cottager has a right to cut turf on the mountain; the farmers give them wool at sheep-shearing; their cottages are well supplied with bacon, and many poach the streams for salmon, and the moors for game. But they have never seen a higher order of civilization, and though they have the means to live respectably, they prefer from ignorance the degraded social condition above described. Nor is this confined to the labouring population. The farmers, who might raise the standard of domestic comfort and civilization, although they live well and dress in superfine cloth, are content to inhabit huts scarcely less dark, dirty and comfortless.

Report on Education in Wales, 1847,3, Appendix, 136. This report is famous for its virulent attack on the standard of education in Wales and its branding of the poorer classes as ignorant and immoral.

the lesser gentry who occupied most of the houses having more than one hearth in 1662, although not all who belonged to this social class lived in such houses. There were in all only nine houses with more than one hearth—one with as many as ten—but as many as ll6 which paid the tax on a single hearth, together with a further unknown number of occupiers exempted from payment on grounds of poverty. Some idea of the size of this last category may be had from the statistics for the county of Pembrokeshire.

According to the returns for 1670, paupers' houses accounted for 46.8 per cent of the households; and 80.5 per cent of all the houses in the county (excluding the town of Haverfordwest) had only one hearth. For the vast majority of the population the single hearth must have dominated domestic life, especially in the winter months. To have a second heated room, with the privacy and separation of functions which that implied, was the prerogative of only a small proportion of the population. The dominance of the heated hall was such that even when parlours were included in the estate farmhouses built in the nineteenth century (in Anglesey, for example), they were generally unused by the family, as were the front doors intended to give access to them.

The single-room cottage

At the lower end of the social scale the single-room cottage was frequently the workplace of some or all of the family, as well as its habitation. A striking description by S.J. Pratt in 1797 of a fisherman's cottage in Barmouth, Merioneth, refers to the family of fourteen who occupied the mud-walled thatched hovel consisting only of a single room. Most of the occupants of the cottage were engaged in some useful activity or other when he visited it. The father was busy making nets, the mother shaving a local innkeeper, the eldest son weaving ribbons, the eldest daughter weaving cloth, the second son mending a petticoat, the second daughter combing the hair of the fourth who was knitting stockings. The sixth daughter was baking bread, the seventh making broth, the eighth rocking the cradle of the youngest with her foot and dangling another in her arms while the fifth was at the spinning wheel. There were three miserable beds, apparently box beds, and also a straw bed; there was no other furniture in the house. No doubt in a farming community the older children would have been in service and would have lived on their employers' premises. Numerous later descriptions reveal just how over-crowded some of these cottages were. Sir Henry Jones describes his home in Llangernyw, Denbighshire, in the 1850s, a nineteenth-century cottage which is still standing, as having a living room measuring ten feet by ten in which all the cooking was done, the meals eaten and visitors entertained. Seven persons ate all their meals there, in relays, except on Sundays when they all dined at the same time, one or two, perhaps, sitting on the doorstep with their plates on their knees, if the weather was fine. The father's workshop—he was a shoemaker by trade—was next door.

Farm kitchens, servants and the stable-loft

Farm kitchens were generally larger and could accommodate the servants at meal times. There was considerable formality as the servants entered the room in order of seniority, led by the *hwsmon* or head servant who presided over the meal, cut and handed round the bread. It was he, too, who signified the end of the meal by

The stable loft at Hendre Wen Farm near Llanrwst in the Vale of Conwy.

34

closing his knife with a click, and leading the servants out of the house. Even the men's caps were hung in the same order in the lobby leading to the kitchen! The family would eat its meal separately in the adjacent 'little parlour' where visiting craftsmen were also fed—but not at the same time as the family. The farmer, however, seated by a small round table at the opposite side of the kitchen to the long table occupied by the servants, would remain in the kitchen to hear reports of the work in progress. In the upland sheep-grazing areas of inland Caernarfonshire a different tradition existed, namely that a shepherd had a right to eat at the same table as the family. In the western coastal districts of Wales the unmarried male servants who partook of the meals in the farm kitchens were generally accommodated in the unheated lofts over the stables and not in the houses. The paradox of the unoccupied parlour and the outdoor sleeping quarters for the men servants did not strike the nineteenth-century Anglesey farmer as unusual in any way, and life in the stable-loft, despite the primitive conditions, had its advantages, especially the independence enjoyed and the freedom to roam the countryside at night. Each of the stable-lofts in turn became the meeting place for the farm servants of a neighbourhood, where a rough-and-ready entertainment to the accompaniment of the accordion or the jews' harp could be enjoyed, and traditional stories, songs and ballads heard. In fact the stable-loft, in those districts of Gwynedd and Dyfed where it was to be found, rivalled the hearth as a focus of informal entertainment.

Winter nights, 'amser gwylad' and the crafts of the hearth

It was during the long winter evenings that the hearth came into its own as the scene of those numerous household chores and domestic crafts which enabled a family to make both ends meet. The change-over from the summer routine to that of winter was associated in mid-Wales with local fairs held in late September. The night of *Ffair Capel Coch*, which was held on 25 September in Llanlleonfel, Breconshire, after everybody had returned from the fair, was the traditional occasion in that district to light the first candle and to eat supper by its light. In Cardiganshire it was *Ffair Gŵyl y Grog* held on 26 September (Holy Rood Day) that marked the beginning of *amser gwylad*, which may be roughly translated as 'time to keep a vigil', or of the time to begin to *cadw dechreunos*, that is, 'to spend (or keep) the evening'. Similar

'Cadw dechreunos' in Eifionydd

The men would chop gorse—the machine was turned by hand—and care for the animals until eight o'clock, and after they had come to the house there would be not tea but flummery for them. For two hours after supper there would be three spinning-wheels at work, and the three daughters were very skilled at spinning with them. The old women would knit stockings and the old man would relate stories to his friends about catching foxes, and tales about the feats of strong men. For example, how Huw Byning carried nine hundredweight of lead to the top of the church tower in Clynnog; how his own sister, who was very nimble, could run up the steep hill from Cybi's Well to Cerrigllwydion field in one breath, that is, without stopping; and also how the farmer of Tyddyn-yr-onnen went to Pwllheli with small horses unaccustomed to work, and how they jibbed at Nant-y-stigallt. The farmer of Tyddyn-yr-onnen who was extremely strong said to the horses, 'You rotten old carcases', placed his shoulder under the axle and carried the load. Since there was spinning going on in the house, the story was told of going to Menai Bridge Fair to sell *swyaeth*, that is, flannel, blankets and home-spun cloth. On another evening candles were made from home-produced tallow—enough for the need of the family for a year. At times, towards the end of the year, the men would make ropes by the light of the candle. On another evening, rush-peeling would be taking place ... As you approached the house in those days in the evening it would be the sound of the spinning-wheel which would draw your attention, or Pero, the dog, snoring; but today it is the piano which is heard in many houses, and the girls are much more proficient in piano-playing than spinning or peeling rushes.

Cymru, 28 (1905), 261–4. (Translated).

dates were observed in other parts of Wales; a native of Llanuwch-llyn, Merioneth, born in 1844, records the practice in that district, but unfortunately had forgotten the precise details. The significance of the occasion, near the time of the autumn equinox, is that knitting, whilst seated around the hearth after the day's work had been completed, could now begin. The *noson weu* (knitting night), which was an informal assembly of neighbours who met, usually on moonlit nights, in the various houses of a neighbourhood in turn, was an important economic and cultural institution in the moorland communities. Woollen hose, knitted by people of all ages, we are told in 1816, was

a staple commodity, forming the greatest part of the commerce of this county of Merioneth. ... This is a source of useful employment, and a happy mode of procuring a livelihood for the poor whom it is common to meet on the roads, travelling upon other business, busily at work with their knitting needles; and no conversation, or any slight occurrence, can divert them from this object of their industry.

However, the Revd Walter Davies, writing at this time, estimated that in Cardiganshire a woman might produce four pairs of stockings a week, each pair weighing about half a pound, costing 5*d.* for the wool and selling for 8*d.* in the market in Tregaron, thus bringing in an income of 1*s.* a week, which although small was 'the only means of subsistence within reach of the poorer sort of females all over this extensive tract'. In north Wales, 'the profit of manufacture is a *mere trifle* and would never answer, were not the knitting of such the occupation of their leisure hours, in walking or by the fireside on a long winter's night—without expense of candle and the means of instructing children'. Knitting was, as Davies suggests, a means of combining work and pleasure in a sociable evening spent on the hearth. In Breconshire, the making of spoons and ladles, brooms and baskets, and similar household articles, by the menfolk, generally accompanied the knitting by the womenfolk. There would often be a competition, supervised by one of the men, to see who could knit a measured fathom of yarn quickest.

The story-telling tradition

In other areas, such as Llanaelhaearn, Caernarfonshire, the *pilnos* or peeling night, when neighbours assembled to dress hemp and card wool (and originally, no doubt to peel rushes in the preparation of rushlights, as the name suggests), was an important factor in keeping alive the tradition of story-telling in the district, according to the Celtic scholar Sir John Rhŷs. *Pigo'r pilnos*, the Anglesey custom, was similarly associated with hemp dressing, in spite of its name. Apart from story-telling, the asking of riddles was a common diversion at these informal evening gatherings. In Llanfrothen, Merioneth, it is recorded that a man used to visit the various houses in the parish to read the Welsh prose classic *Drych y Prif Oesoedd* by Theophilus Evans to those who were assembled on the hearth. It was the purely oral tradition, however, which flourished in these fireside meetings. 'Robin Bryn-Moel' (1825–85) who lived in the Dolwyddelan district of Caernarfonshire, is a good example of the tradition-bearer who found his audience in these fireside gatherings. We are told that 'Robin had scores of old humorous tales which were recited on winter evenings on the hearths of the rural areas of Wales, and I can say unhesitantly that I never heard his equal in the art of telling them—as natural as running water. He was given a gentleman's welcome when he visited the houses of his old acquaintances everywhere, especially in Dolwyddelan, his native district'. As was said of the repertoire of 'Ioan Glan Lledr', who was born in the same year and in the same parish, 'our ancestors only had stories of this sort to entertain the family on the hearth during the long winter evenings, without any light, except that which came from a blazing fire of wood or peat'. The atmosphere of these evening gatherings, with their reminiscences of local events, is recaptured in an account written in 1905 of life at Maen-llwyd farm, Llangybi, Caernarfonshire, in the middle of the nineteenth century which is reproduced on page 36.

It is easy to understand how these evening gatherings became the occasions for a *noson lawen* (merry night) with informal competitions in the composing and singing of impromptu verses in which all present were expected to participate.

Nos Calan Gaeaf

Apart from these work-based customs, the hearth was the scene of divination on *Nos Calan Gaeaf*. All Hallows Eve, or Hollantide as it was sometimes called, was celebrated on 31 October, and as the traditional beginning of the winter half of the year in the old Celtic calendar, it was believed that supernatural influences were intensified, enabling the future to be foretold from various omens. Many forms of divination were connected with the church building: one might see who was going to die in the parish in the forthcoming year if one looked through the keyhole of the church door at midnight. But not only were spirits abroad in the countryside and ghosts of dead persons to be met at every stile;

This glazed earthenware puzzle jug, dated '1711', was probably made at Ewenni, Glamorgan.

the forces of the other world were active in the home itself on this evening. The procession homeward from the bonfire associated with the occasion in Merioneth would be followed by a convivial gathering in the house. The traditional meal eaten on this occasion consisted of *stwmp naw rhyw* (a mash of nine sorts); with the nine vegetables comprising this dish a wedding ring was carefully concealed, and whoever found the ring with his spoon as he ate the meal, would be the first of those present to be married. In Carmarthenshire, the wassail bowl made its appearance on this evening, as well as the puzzle jug, with its perforated rim, from which one had to drink without spilling the spiced drink it contained. Many of the games played had a divinatory element such as peeling apples with a knife without breaking the ribbon of peel, and then discerning the initial letter of one's future spouse from the way in the peel fell when thrown over the shoulder. Nuts (or ivy leaves) cast into the fire foretold the future from the way they burned. A blindfolded person could, by dipping his hands into one of three bowls placed before him, discover whether the future would bring death or matrimony to him. Such diversions survived as harmless entertainment long after the belief in their significance in foretelling the future had ceased.

Ritual entry to the house and wedding customs

Apart from activities on the hearth itself, the winter half of the year, in particular, was the period when a number of peripatetic customs took place. Social life in Wales was most active, as was suggested in the first chapter, not at the centre, but at the extremities, not in the towns and villages, but in the isolated farmsteads and cottages of the countryside. Normally, one gained access to the house without any formality. The visitors called out the usual question 'Are there people here?' and let themselves in: easy access and hospitality went together, and food would be offered to all who called. In some districts a place was set at the table for *Morus Trawsfynydd*—'Morris from over the mountain'—the unexpected guest. In Dyfed, the marriage bidder, whose task was to invite people to weddings and to remind them of the wedding debts which they were to repay to the young couple, was entitled by tradition to walk unannounced into every house in the district, and to strike the floor three times with his staff of office to inform everybody of his presence before beginning his formal address of invitation. All the evidence suggests that in normal everyday experience entry into the house was easy, informal and unrestricted. The hearth tradition in this dispersed cultural pattern flourished on the basis of this fact.

There were, however, special occasions when entry to the house was formalized, even ritualized. One such occasion in Dyfed was on the eve of a wedding when the custom of 'setting forth the marriage chamber' took place. The womenfolk came together on this occasion in order to prepare the wedding feast which was to be held the following day. This was the evening, too, when all the furniture belonging to the young couple was brought into the new home, and there is evidence which suggests that in some districts a recognized order in which the various items were to be carried into the house was observed, and that that the ceremony itself was supervised by the two mothers. However, the most dramatic form which this ritual entry to the house took was the mock poetic contest between those inside the house, and those outside seeking entry. This took place on the wedding day, when it constituted a special form of the 'quintain' or ritual hindrance of the wedding, when the 'young man's party' (the *shigowts* or 'seek-outs') came to fetch the bride. Obstacles of all kinds were placed in the farmyard and lanes to prevent access to the house; the door was bolted, and it was there in the doorway, through the closed door, that the contest in verse took place. Local characters who were well-known versifiers sometimes gave assistance in the drawn-out contest which would involve singing several verses and responses, before the door was opened and the visitors allowed in. The 'seek-outs' sometimes succeeded in carrying off the bride on horseback, only to be overtaken on the way to church.

Door-to-door winter customs

The ritual entry to the house was also to be found in a highly structured form in some of the folk customs, particularly variants of wassailing, belonging to the winter half of the year. These customs had in common with each other and with certain other calendar customs, the practice of carrying from house to house a ritual object—a horse's head, a wassail bowl, a new year's gift, new year's water (freshly drawn from the well in order to sprinkle the occupants), a wren on a bier, a *perllan* ('orchard' or tray decorated with apples and a miniature bird), egg clappers, and a *crochon Crewys* (Lenten crock).

In their simplest forms, these customs involved displaying the ritual object at the door, having first sung or knocked so as to draw attention or greet the householder. At one extreme this took

Souling in north Wales: a nineteenth-century account and explanation

Little by little the service for the dead became dear and expensive; and for that reason there was no hope for the souls of the poor to come out of purgatory more than from hell; because they themselves when they died had nothing to leave to the priests to pray for them; and their living friends did not have the necessary gifts to give in order to purchase the prayers and intercession of the priests to save the souls of their relatives from the pains of purgatory: and it is probably this which led to begging on the first of November. Because it was the poor, so that they would have something to offer to the priests on the Feast of All Souls, namely the second day of November, for praying for their relatives and saving them from purgatory, who used to go on the first day [of the month] as though on a preparatory feast day, around their rich neighbours to request and receive their gifts and assistance in this charitable work, as they thought. The one who went around, whoever he was, was called *cennad y meirw* or one coming from or on behalf of the dead to ask for help; and the custom in some places was to make cakes to be given to the messengers of the dead when they came around, and to call them the bread or the food of the messengers of the dead. These cakes are called by our neighbours the English in some of the counties of England 'soul cakes' ... Perhaps the word *solod* ... is a corruption of this word ... As to the method of asking for these gifts, the old people in this district say that it was like this—'Deca, Deca, dowch i'r drws, a rhowch ... i gennad y meirw'. [Deca, Deca, come to the door, and give ... to the messenger of the dead]. And then, if nothing was received, they would say, 'Deca, Deca, o dan y drws, a phen y wraig yn siwtrws' [Deca, Deca, under the door, and the wife's head smithereens']. ... But thank God, those dark days have passed for us Welsh.

Y Gwyliedydd, 1823, 215. (Translated)

the form of socially approved begging on (or usually before) feast days. For example, *hel solod* (souling), also known as *hel bwyd cennad y meirw* (collecting the food of the messenger of the dead), took place in many parts of the country on All Souls' Eve (1 November) when soul cakes were collected from house to house. This custom is thought to be derived from the collections made for the purpose of releasing the souls of the dead from purgatory in pre-Reformation times.

'Thomasing' (*yta*) took place on St Thomas's Day (21 December) when women went from door to door to collect corn or flour to make loaves and cakes for Christmas. The collecting of *calennig* (a new penny in recent times) on New Year's Day; *blawta a blonega* (collecting flour and fats on Shrove Tuesday) and the collecting of eggs before Easter are other examples of sanctioned begging by the poor and, latterly, by children. In Dyfed, as we saw in the previous chapter, those families helping in the harvest and on the potato field felt they had a special claim to small gifts of this kind. Seventeenth-century Anglesey in times of dearth was pestered by 'idle devouring drones' who, having corn and food of their own in another part of the island, dressed in rags and begged from door to door for a month or two 'that their store at home may be better spared'. Others, 'well apparell'd' had 'a kind of set speech, and rhetoricall oration to be delivered at every door, and can sing out some odd song withall'—a description which fits some of the folk customs of a later period. At the opposite extreme to this scarcely disguised form of begging, greeting and wishing the householder and his family well could be spun out in a highly elaborate way, with musical and poetical embellishments, the aim being not so much the collection of food or money, as to enjoy the company and hospitality of the household.

The 'Mari Lwyd'

The *Mari Lwyd* (lit. 'Grey Mary') of south Wales, which is probably the best known of these customs, belonged to the Christmas season and the New Year. It consisted of taking from door to door a horse's skull covered with a white sheet and decorated with colourful ribbons; this was carried by a man concealed under the sheet who could operate the jaw and make it snap. The party, normally dressed up as Sergeant, Merryman, Punch and Judy, led the *Mari* to the door of the house and engaged in a poetic contest, often singing as many as fifteen verses before they were

43

A Glamorgan Mari Lwyd *and its party.*

eventually allowed to enter. The *Mari,* on entering the house, would run wildly after the girls snapping at them with its jaws until the time came to enjoy the food and drink offered in plenty. The origin of this custom has been variously explained. It was, however, clearly a form of wassailing, and one of the elaborate earthenware wassail bowls made at the Ewenni pottery in the Vale of Glamorgan was often carried around by the *Mari Lwyd* party as well as by other wassailers in the district who did not take the horse's head with them on their visits.

The 'wren house'

The 'wren house' of Pembrokeshire was another ritual object carried from house to house to the accompaniment of verses sung at the door, this time on Twelfth Night. The body of a wren, placed in a small box decorated with ribbons to serve as its bier, and resting on four poles, was borne by four men ostentatiously groaning under the huge weight of their burden. The verses, sometimes sung in the form of question and answer, varied from district to district, and often ended, as did so many of these songs, with a request to be allowed into the house. The prolonged Christmas season to which the custom belonged—and the Roman *Lupercalia*

*This wren house, probably the only surviving example, was made in 1869
by Richard Cobb, sexton, Marloes, Pembrokeshire, like those he made sixty
years earlier.*

which preceded it—was associated with the idea of the world
turned upside down, its normal behaviour and values being temporarily set aside: just as in religion the new-born Christ-child
in his manger was worshipped as God, so in this secular custom
the tiny wren was treated ceremonially as the King of birds.

Candlemas

One of the most elaborate examples among Welsh folk customs
of this ritual embellishment of wassailing was recorded in Gwynedd in the eighteenth century and related to Candlemas, the Feast
of the Purification of the Virgin Mary, known in Welsh as *Gŵyl
Fair y Canhwyllau* and celebrated on 2 February. The first 'carol'
sung by the party as it reached the door was the *carol yn drws*
(carol at the door) which kept to the usual pattern of a ritual
poetic contest; after the party had been allowed to enter the house
a second carol was sung, this time requesting a chair to be placed
in the middle of the floor, and a young girl, with a little child
to sit on her knee, to be found to represent the Virgin Mary and
Child. After singing this 'chair carol' (*carol cadair*), the party then

45

filed in procession around the chair and its occupants, having asked in yet another carol for the wassail to be served from the hand of the man of the house so that the young girl seated in the chair could be 'pledged'. She was then proferred the bowl and asked to drink, and also to give some to the young child as the carol was being sung; she was then to pass the bowl to the carollers, rise from her chair and move away. The carollers then drank their share of the wassail, not without some risk of singeing their eyebrows and whiskers, for the bowl (as they state in their carol) was decorated with lighted candles or tapers attached to its rim. One Caernarfonshire example of a carol (or series of carols) sung in the course of a Candlemas visit called for five different ballad tunes, the singing of each of which marked a stage in the enactment of the ritual. As in the *Mari Lwyd* custom in the opposite corner of Wales, a carol of thanks was sung at the end of the feasting —'a wassail carol on departing'. One is left with the impression that Candlemas singing (*Canu Gŵyl Fair* or *Canu gwirod*) consisted of an orchestrated sequence of secular carols, each of which prolonged the musical and poetical celebration far beyond the original ritual of entry. A native tradition of contest in verse, which was a central part of the hearth entertainment itself, seems to have been linked with the riddle tradition and the performing of feats, and applied to the gaining of access on a ritual occasion. Some of the secular carols recorded by Richard Morris in Anglesey in the early eighteenth century belong to this latter tradition, as well as the popular folk song *Cyfri'r Geifr* (Counting the goats), and similar tongue-twisting verses.

Marking the coming of spring

The end of *amser gwylad* came in March and was associated in Cardiganshire and the neighbouring parts of Breconshire with *Nos Ffair Caron*, the evening of 16 March, when the fair was held in Tregaron. That evening the maid symbolically handed back a candle to her mistress, signifying that from then on the family would retire to bed before dark and rise with the lark in the morning. It was said that in some households the candle returned was the same one as had been handed out the previous September. On Old St David's Day, 12 March, in the Gwaun valley of north Pembrokeshire, the wax candle in the candle-holder on the table was replaced by a wooden candle as a sign that it was no longer necessary to eat supper by candlelight. This was expressed in the couplet

'Nos Ŵyl Ddewi fe gaiff Ben
Fwyta'i swper wrth ganwyll bren'.

(St David's Eve and Ben shall / Eat his supper by a wooden
candle)

This was, in fact, one of the few ways in which St David's Day
affected the daily life of the countryside, and like other feast days
its celebration had been altered by the change in the Calendar
in 1751. To farm labourers in nineteenth-century Dyfed, too, this
was the time of the year when they became entitled to three meals
a day, until Michaelmas when they would revert to two meals
until the following Old St David's Day.

The coming of spring also affected mealtimes in other ways,
and it is recorded in Breconshire that when the first bracken head
was seen sprouting from the soil it would be taken to the farmwife
as a sign that bread and milk should be placed on the table the
last thing at night for those members of the household who would
henceforth rise at four or five in the morning to start work on
the farm; they could not be expected to wait until the usual time
of eight o'clock for their breakfast. In the same district also it
was customary to take an hour's rest after dinner, and the sign
that the time of the year had come to begin this practice was
when the leaf of the alder was as big as a shilling, when it would
be taken to be shown to the farmer. The routine in the woollen
factories of the country districts was also affected by the lengthen-
ing of the day, and the young people of Tal-y-bont, Cardiganshire,
on an unspecified day in March, when working by candlelight
in the factory was discontinued for the summer, would assemble
in the middle of the village and form a procession to walk through
the street singing:

Ffarwel i'r hen ganhwyllau, ffarwel i wylad nos,
Ffarwel i fyned adref rhwng naw a deg y nos—hwre, hwre,
    hwre,
Ffarwel i'r hen ganhwyllau, fe ddaeth y Jiwbili,
A pheidiwch a rhyfeddu mai canu'r ydym ni—hwre, hwre,
    hwre.

(Farewell to the old candles, farewell to 'keeping the evenings'
/ Farewell to going home between nine and ten o'clock at
night—hurray, hurray, hurray,/ Farewell to the old candles,
the Jubilee has come / And don't be surprised that we are
singing—hurray, hurray, hurray).

47

Before the introduction of electricity to the workplace and the home, the contrast between winter and summer left a much deeper impression on human experience, and the coming of the long summer evenings, when hearth traditions receded into the background, held out the promise of life in the open air, even though this might entail more toil than leisure.

3 Community Traditions

Charity and hardship

It is not surprising that country people, who were accustomed to help each other in the work on the land, especially at harvest time, and to visit each other's homes during the winter evenings, should have developed communal ways of overcoming the hardship brought about by sudden death or incapacitation, by unexpected economic disaster or natural catastrophe, or by the need to provide for an uncertain future. Before the spread of friendly societies in the nineteenth century, let alone the emergence of the welfare provisions of the modern state heralded by the appearance of the workhouse after 1834, the parish dole, various local charities and begging were the only choices open to the poor who had fallen on hard times. St Thomas's Day, in particular, perhaps because it occurred a few days before Christmas, continued well into the nineteenth century as an occasion for charity. On that day in 1881, for example, Sir Watkin Williams Wynn of Rhiwabon, Denbighshire, the leading landowner in north Wales, gave away twenty-one pieces of cloth (each large enough to make a coat), sixty-five pieces of flannel, each measuring three yards, and one shilling each to the infirm of the district. It is interesting to note, also, that such philanthropy was often institutionalized and perpetuated in the form of bequests, so that a person accustomed to giving charity on that day could ensure that his almsgiving continued after his own lifetime. Such almsgiving had long been an ingrained virtue of gentility. At Gwydir, Llanrwst, home of Sir John Wynn, a prominent landowner in Caernarfonshire, one of the servants, a porter, was reported to his employer in 1623 'for being bitter in speech to the poor who came for alms, and for beating them with a long rod about their bare legs and feet so that they kept away, which was contrary to Sir John's wishes'. Seventeenth-century gentlemen might not have followed Jeremy Taylor's advice that they should, for the benefit of their souls, give their alms in person, but they would at least have, as did Chancellor Wynne of Bodewryd, Anglesey, in the following century, a 'chest for the poor's dole', even though it was, in this instance, located in the servants' hall. This item of furniture no doubt corresponds to the *cist gymorth* (assistance chest) to which

William Morris of Holyhead, in the same county, refers in a letter dated 1762. Begging was also linked to the other major festivals of the church calendar, and the ranks of the beggars were swollen during the distress which almost invariably followed a bad harvest before the importing of foreign food on a large scale after the middle of the last century.

It was not only the poor who were affected when the harvest failed, but it was always they who suffered most. After the disastrous summer of 1816, the farmers of the upland area between Tregaron and Ysbyty Cynfyn in north Cardiganshire were forced to buy seed-corn, but found it impossible to do so because they were unable to sell their animals to get ready money; nor could they borrow money for this purpose. Most of the agricultural labourers were thus idle for six months and 'went on the parish'; but the parish could not maintain them by levying a rate on the farmers in the usual way because of the hardship of the latter. The farmers (as well as the labourers) were unable to buy the corn brought by sea to Carmarthen, Cardigan and Aberystwyth, and the entire population went without food for two days at a time, or was reduced to eating plants such as nettles to keep alive. The wet summer was followed by a long, hard winter, and this was when many of the inhabitants of the Builth district of Breconshire were forced to buy coal for the first time, the peat which they had harvested not having dried well enough to burn on their hearths; they were also unable to plant their potatoes early to obtain a supply of food for the beginning of summer; and since the pasture was poor in quality, the condition of the cattle suffered, and there was little prospect of butter. The failure of the harvest thus had a cumulative effect on the economy, and affected the entire community, driving it to rely on its own devices to alleviate hardship among its less fortunate members during such times of distress, as well as in the course of everyday life.

'Cyfarfod cymorth'

One institution which was of direct benefit to the poor was the *cyfarfod cymorth* or 'assistance meeting' which derived its name from the medieval *cymortha* or exaction levied by a lord for his own benefit. Although abolished by the Acts of Union of 1535–6, the practice survived in a more benevolent form and under various names for over 300 years. The term *cymorth*, used in this specialized sense, appears to have been more common in the north of the country; in Llanwynno, Glamorgan, in contrast, it was used, as in *cymorth aredig* (ploughing assistance), for those occasions of co-operative work on the land, when there would often be fierce competition, particularly during haymaking, to discover who was the most skilful. In the Vale of Clwyd, the clergyman received *cymorth* or assistance during the corn or peat harvest, and farmers hauled anything he might require without charge. *Cymorth glo* (coal assistance) referred to the custom in the same district of hauling the blacksmith's coal free of charge. However, in Llangollen, Denbighshire, in 1822, the practice was described in general terms as 'an assembly of neighbours upon the mutual principle of mutual assistance and good fellowship', but took the following local form.

> The *cyfarvod cymorth* was a meeting held for the benefit of a poor person, at whose house or that of a neighbour, a number of young women, mostly servants, used to meet, by permission of their respective employers, in order to give day's work, either in spinning or knitting, according as there was need of their assistance; and towards the close of the day, when their task was ended, dancing and singing were usually introduced, and the evening spent with glee and conviviality.

The occasion was enlivened by the giving of love tokens by the suitors of the participants—usually cakes or silver spoons highly decorated with flowers, with a sprig of hazel, the symbol of rejection, added if the lover intended to break off the relationship. 'These pledges were handed to the respective lasses by the different *Caisars*, or Merry Andrews,—persons dressed in disguise for the occasion, who, in their turn, used to take each his young woman by the hand to an adjoining department, where he would deliver the *pwysi* or nose-gay, as it was called, and immediately retire upon having mentioned the giver's name'. The *cymorth* might also be held in the evening, when the servants were not expected to ask leave of their employers to attend.

'Cwrw bach' or 'bid ale'
In many parts of Wales the occasion was considerably enlivened in another way, namely, through the sale of ale specially brewed by the householder. The *cwrw bach* ('small beer', from the nature of the drink sold) or 'bid ale' as it was sometimes known, was purely a fund-raising social occasion, its profit augmented in various ways. *Meth* (for *medd*, 'mead') and (in Cardiganshire) *tabletsh* (a kind of beer) were other names by which this meeting was

The 'cwrw bach' and the Methodist preacher

In Glamorgan, especially in the industrial areas, people usually held what they called a *cwrw bach*. This consisted of somebody making beer in his house so as to raise a sum of money for the rent or a difficult time of grief &c. This had become a general custom among almost everybody, and had become extremely corrupt. They would go there for the benefit of the family, and as a result everybody thought it was their duty to drink as much as possible; and he who spent the most money was accounted the most honourable on that occasion. In another part of the house, some fifteen to twenty of the fair sex would be enjoying themselves in a *Clwb Te* (Tea Club) in order to show their fondness for and sympathy with the distressed family. This place, as was previously suggested, was a very unpleasant court for anybody to have his personal, family or general cause tried. ... It happened one night, when Siencyn was passing a certain house, that there was a *cwrw bach* there; and he heard the business of the wet meeting in full swing. He wondered what he should do. He stood and thought, 'How can I give this beast a mortal blow?' Something inside him said, 'Go in, Shanco.' Into their midst he went at last; he took off his hat and looked about him, until the attention of the whole meeting was on him. Then he said to them, 'You will all be in hell in no time, every one of you.' The people were frightened and would have fled if they could; and to many of them Siencyn was perfectly well known. In the middle of everything he said, 'Let us pray.' He prayed with such unconquerable strength until nearly everybody in the place was stunned. Anyway, they had enough strength to go from there, every one of them, before the prayer ended, for there was nobody else there besides himself when he rose from his knees. That was how this jollification was broken up.

Edward Matthews, *Hanes Bywyd Siencyn Penhydd: neu Mr Jenkin Thomas, Penhydd, Morganwg*, ?1850, 51–2. (Translated) known, according to what was offered to drink. Mead, which was sweeter, was regarded as more respectable (and possibly more intoxicating) than small beer; it was also cheaper to produce. To avoid breaking the law, no charge was made for the beer itself, but the *pice*, or small cakes, which accompanied it were sold at a high price. Such meetings were widely supported, particularly by young men and women, and there would frequently be rivalry among the latter to see who could take home the most *pice* as an indication of their popularity with the opposite sex. Singing and dancing to the music of the harp was a common feature of the *cwrw bach* in the Aman Valley, on the border of Glamorgan and Carmarthenshire, the performers being rewarded in kind. Raffles were held for prizes such as a pig, a sheep or a watch, names being collected during the preceding weeks. It was often a friend of the householder, rather than the householder himself who discreetly received the various contributions. In Cardiganshire, two vessels were placed on the kitchen table, the larger filled by the housewife, and the lesser by one of the neighbours, who, after drinking the health of the housewife, served all those present with the lesser vessel—for which one shilling was paid—until the larger vessel was emptied. This was then replenished, and the same procedure repeated, another neighbour taking over the serving. These meetings, although their charitable purpose of assisting a family in need was freely acknowledged, were criticized, in the words of a Breconshire biographer, as 'a breeding place of immorality and licentiousness [which] spread its infectious influence' through the district. That this was sometimes the case is borne out by a newspaper report of a paternity suit in 1859 from which it appears that the defendant, a butcher from Burry Port, Carmarthenshire, and his male friend, had called at a house to look for girls to take to a *cwrw bach* elsewhere. This was being held to benefit the householder's daughter, the putative father of whose child had run away. The young people were at the *cwrw bach*, amusing themselves and drinking from nine o'clock in the evening until three in the morning, the alleged act taking place after they had returned. A reference to an earlier meeting of this kind in Dolgellau, Merioneth, in 1780, suggests that some form of segregation took place with 'the graver sort' being entertained in the kitchen of a well-to-do neighbour, while the 'gayer' sort danced in the house of the widow who had brewed the ale and who received sixpence from each person attending. In the Vale of Glamorgan, with its more hierarchical tradition, the *cwrw bach* was linked, in one recorded instance which had become an annual event, to the Hunt, the Master of the Hounds being asked to arrange a meet outside an old woman's cottage. Many came besides the regular followers, and most of the provisions, such as malt, oatmeal, cheese, tea and sugar, were donated by the families, who arrived later on horseback for the tea served in the afternoon. Guests were expected to leave sixpence on a large plate on the kitchen table. In the evening, servants and maids came, sometimes from many miles away. There would be beer on tap, a bottle of rhubarb wine would be opened, and there would be singing and dancing to the music of the harp. Such convivial occasions might end in over-indulgence, and as one local historian wrote of Llansawel, Carmarthenshire, 'it was often the case that matters grew from jest to earnest, and, to put it lightly, those who had come for fun left in a quarrelsome mood. Through this the *cwrw bach* has been supplemented by tea parties, got up with the same object.'

Fund raising at the 'pastai'

A related custom was the *pastai* (pasty or pie) which was often held, not in a private house but in a tavern. It seems to have been particularly popular in Glamorgan and adjacent parts of Breconshire and Gwent, and is referred to as *pastai wawdd* in a list of the customs of Glamorgan compiled by Iolo Morganwg (1747–1826, creator of the modern *Gorsedd* of Bards and recorder of folk traditions). Like *cwrw gwawdd*, which he also mentions, the name indicates that attendance was by invitation. The Ynys-y-bŵl *pastai* in Glamorgan was held in the beginning of August each year, when the beneficiary would go round the parish beforehand to invite, and also to receive 'a little bacon, or oatmeal, a bit of salted beef, and some wool, too, in some places'. A similar *pastai* was held at Tafarn-isaf, Mountain Ash, and another annually in Llanwynno church, in the same parish, probably in the adjacent hostelry. In the upper Swansea valley, Tafarn y Garreg, the Gwyn Arms, the Mount Pleasant and the Ancient Briton, each had its *pastai* during the first week in October—-probably a relic of the patronal festival—and we are told that everybody would attend, or at least send a dish with a shilling in it to receive a portion of the *pastai*. Many 'doublers' (platters) of the meat of the best wether available from local farmers were previously prepared, the dishes being covered with a delectable pastry. A female 'bidder' was sent around every house a fortnight beforehand to invite guests, using the following set phrase, 'Mr and Mrs Jeffries of such-and-such Tavern invite you to a *pastai* to be held on such-and-such. A harper will be in attendance; one shilling a head.' The local saying was, 'dechrau'r wythnos, henoed; canol wythnos, canol oed; a gweddill yr wythnos i'r ieuainc.' (The beginning of the week, old people; middle of the week, the middle aged; and the rest of the week for the young people).

Although the guests were charged for the food, the profit came from the sale of drink. An earlier description of the *pastai gwawdd* of south-east Wales, published in 1824, is more reminiscent of the *cwrw bach*, being held in a private house for the occupier's benefit, although a bidder was employed, which does not seem to have happened when a *cwrw bach* was held. Apart from general poverty (or widowhood), the immediate reasons given for holding these charitable meetings included the loss of an animal, the inability to pay the rent, a long illness or incapacity resulting from an accident, and the maintenance of an illegitimate child. There were, in addition, two other important family events with which special forms of these gatherings were held, namely, death and marriage, which call for separate discussion .

Funerals and community support
In addition to the personal grief which it involved, death might well mean immediate, if not permanent, hardship for a family lacking any substantial resources, and *talu siot*, paying 'shot', was one of several ways of helping a bereaved household. After a funeral, the mourners, who were always numerous in the traditional community, would retire to the *tŷ'n llan*, or hostelry in the vicinity of the parish church. There, they would contribute towards the 'shot', men generally paying a shilling and women sixpence. For this they received beer and cakes, respectively, the drink being brought to the tables in jugs. The names of all who had contributed to the 'shot' were recorded, and the list subsequently handed over to the nearest relatives of the deceased. All were expected to contribute, but it was not necessary to stay to get the full value of the contribution. When the first contribution had been expended in drink and tobacco, the person in charge would cry out. 'Y mae'r tŷ yn rhydd!' (The house is free!) whereupon a second round of contributions would commence, and so on. Another version of the 'shot' took place when the mourners were too poor to bear the cost of the funeral; a collection would be made, this time outside the house, a plate having being placed

on a basin, and the money then 'shot' off the plate into the basin 'so that the bereaved family might know what each mourner gave'. Although this might seem to explain the name given to the practice, this version of *talu siot* resembles another funeral custom, *danfon offrwm*, found in another part of Wales, which is discussed in Chapter 5.

Weddings and biddings

The other major occasion when a family needed outside support was in setting up home on marriage. The 'bidding', which followed the wedding in many parts of south Wales, is the most interesting of these money-raising gatherings which might attract hundreds of participants and bring the newly-wed couple a substantial sum of money in the form of gifts and loans. A 'bidder', or *gwahoddwr*, who was usually a well-known local character, would be employed to visit the houses of friend and neighbours, especially those whose weddings and biddings the young couple had attended in the past. His function was to invite all and sundry to the wedding and bidding, and in particular to remind those who owed 'bidding debts' to the young couple to repay them at the forthcoming bidding. The invitation could be given verbally in a set piece which would include both the names of those relatives of the young couple who wished to transfer their own debts to the benefit of the newly-weds, and also a promise to repay any contributions when called for on a similar future occasion. The bidder would be specially dressed in a white apron, or similar distinctive clothes, decorated with ribbons, and. as we have seen, could by tradition enter any house unannounced—a complete contrast to the delayed entry of the wassailers and *Mari Lwyd* during their visits. He would begin his address (or 'rammas') having first drawn attention to the ornamented staff which was the symbol of his office. He might also deliver a 'bidding letter' containing the same information in a more permanent form. His address of invitation might be preceded by a song and a dance so as to bring everybody running to the kitchen in time to to see his act and hear the formal invitation with its reminder of the debts. The visit of the bidder was always a memorable occasion and many versions of his address have been recorded, some in verse, others in prose.

To succeed in his important task the bidder had to be 'well-skilled in the business', quick-witted and with a ready answer', for on his powers of persuasion depended the attendance at the

An idealized portrayal of the bidder in his distinctive head-dress and carrying his decorated staff of office as he invites guests to a bidding. From Peter Roberts, Cambrian Popular Antiquities, *1815.*

bidding and thus the financial support given. Having delivered his invitation, the bidder was entertained to food and drink by the household, and would often return home at night the worse for drink. This hospitality, and small gifts of oatmeal or bread and cheese, were his reward; more affluent farmers might pay the bidder eight to ten shillings for his trouble, but usually the cost was borne collectively by the guests and not by the young couple—an important consideration.

On the day of the bidding itself an account book would be kept by the 'secretary' to record the various gifts, loans and repayments as the sixpences and shillings were placed in a bowl on the table at which the newly-weds sat. Food and drink were served in another room, or outside in an outbuilding cleared for the occasion, where the young people, in particular, congregated. As in the *cwrw bach* the beer might be free and an excessive charge made for the accompanying cakes, the profit, of course, going to the young couple.

It was important from a financial standpoint to attract as many unmarried people as possible, for married people who came to the bidding for the most part came to repay their debts. It was the contributions of the unmarried which were the uncalculable factor, and clearly the more of them there were present, the greater the financial benefit—even though some of their contributions would have to be subsequently repaid. From examples of such accounts as have survived it is possible to estimate the economic importance of the bidding to the 'lower orders' who were among its main supporters in the nineteenth century. For example, from the account book of William Williams of Clwyd-ffwrn, Llanwenog, Cardiganshire, we can deduce that 285 attended his bidding in April 1810, not all of them on the bidding day. Their total contributions amounted to £16. 7s. 6d., of which 101 items amounting to £6. 7s. consisted of bidding debts repaid at the bidding; 156 items amounting to £9. 7s. were new debts incurred by William Williams and subsequently repaid by him at future biddings; a further twenty-four items were bidding payments received by William Williams at his bidding but not recorded as having been subsequently repaid. The sums raised at biddings in Cardiganshire seem on the whole to have been less than those raised in Carmarthenshire and west Glamorgan, but nevertheless constituted a substantial contribution towards the expense of setting up house on getting married, especially when one of the partners came from another locality and decided to hold a separate bidding.

The Bidder's Address

I was desired to call here as a messenger and a bidder. David J. and Ann W. in the parish of Laugharne, the Hundred of Derllys, Co. Carmarthen, encouraged by their friends to make a bidding on Tuesday next; the two young people make their residence in Gosport No. 11, thence to St Michael's Church to be married. The two young people return to the young woman's father and mother's house to dinner. They shall have good beef and cabbage, mutton and turnips, pork and potatoes, roast goose or gant, perhaps both if they are in season, a quart of drink for fourpence, a cake for a penny, clean chairs to sit down upon, clean pipes and tobacco, and attendance of the best; a good song, but if no one will sing, then I'll sing as well as I can; and if no one will attend, I'll attend as well as I can. As a usual custom with us, in Laugharne, is to hold a 'sending gloves' before the wedding, if you'll be pleased to come, or send a waggon or a cart, a horse or a colt, a heifer, a cow and calf, or an ox and a half, or pigs, cocks, hens, geese, goslings, ducks, turkeys, a saddle and bridle, or a child's cradle, or what the house can afford. A great many can help one, but one cannot help a great many. Or send a waggon full of potatoes, a cartload of turnips, a hundred or two of cheeses, a cask of butter, a sack of flour, a winchester of barley, or what you please, for anything will be acceptable; jugs, basins, saucepans, pots and pans, or what you can; throw in five pounds if you like; gridirons, frying pans, tea-kettles, plates and dishes, a lootch [wooden spoon] and dish, spoons, knives and forks, pepperboxes, salt cellars, mustard-pots, or even a penny whistle or a child's cradle. Ladies and gentleman, I was desired to speak this way that all pwyths [payments] due to the young woman's father and mother, grandfather and grandmother, aunts, brothers and sisters, and the same due to the young man's father and mother &c. &c. must be returned to the young people on the above day. So no more at present. If you please to order your butler, or under-servant, to give a quart of drink to the bidder.

Mary Curtis, *The Antiquities of Laugharne, Pendine and their neighbourhoods*, 1880, 210.

A similar impression of the economic importance of the bidding is gained from a different kind of account book which was kept by unmarried persons as a record of the payments made at biddings which they could expect to recover when they themselves got married, or, alternatively, transfer to the benefit of members of their family on similar occasions. A list from the same county at the beginning of the last century reveals the writer to have attended a hundred biddings and parted with the sum of six guineas, paying an average of 1s. 3d. at each bidding. His female relative had paid out £4 at sixty-nine biddings, an average of one shilling. Their servant, incidentally, we learn from other entries, had received £3. 10s. in wages in the year 1803–4, and had attended two biddings paying out 4s. 6d.; in the course of the following year he spent 9s. 6d. at three biddings—nearly one-seventh of his earnings for that year. For this he could expect to receive the equivalent of two or three years' wages when he himself got married, a considerable help when 'making a start in life' (*dechrau eu byd*), as the saying went. This primitive form of hire-purchase, for such it was, allowed the payments to be spread over a considerable period of time and the benefits to be enjoyed when most needed. It was far more important to the labourers, small farmers and craftsmen, who relied on this institution in south-west Wales to finance their marriages, than the exciting chase on horseback to the church on the wedding day, for which every available horse in the district would be used or borrowed, according to an account from the Llanwrtyd, Breconshire, an area where the bidding also flourished.

Wedding races

In north Wales, the situation was rather different, for there the equivalent of the bidding resembled the *talu siot* which accompanied the funeral, and there was nothing like the complicated system of loans and gifts found in the southern counties. In Caernarfonshire and Anglesey the most popular feature of the traditional wedding was the race from the church door, begun immediately the bride had worn her wedding ring during the service, to the house where the wedding feast was to be held, the reward being the wedding cake. On one occasion in Llanllechid, Caernarfonshire, for example, thirty young men ran a distance of four miles in such a race. In Anglesey, Lewis Morris, who curiously made no reference to the race, concisely summarized the rather tempestuous wedding celebrations of the first half of the eighteenth century in his native county: 'they come home from church, dinner custards & paying on a plate drinking woeing, dancing, *campio* (frolicking), each paying his shott, Fighting'.

The 'tŷ unnos'

A somewhat different and specialized form of community co-operation, which did not involve financial contributions but nevertheless depended upon the goodwill of neighbours, concerned the *tŷ unnos*, or house built overnight on an encroachment on the enclosed waste, generally, but not always, in the moorland districts. It was firmly believed that any such building, constructed hastily of turf overnight so that smoke could issue from its chimney the following morning, became the legal property of the builder, together with such land as lay within an axe's throw in each direction. There was no basis in law for such a belief, but this does not seem to have deterred the erection of these 'clod halls' on common land under the pressure of the population growth of the eighteenth century and later. The turf structure was merely

A tŷ unnos *or squatter's cabin in the Welsh Folk Museum, St Fagan's, built as an experiment by architectural students in 1988.*

61

Building a 'tŷ unnos' near Tregaron, Cardiganshire c.1840–70

The first thing was hearing that the carpenter was preparing a door and windows for someone, and there would be much speculation as to who the owner could be. The cottager would prepare a number of necessary things and ask his neighbours to come to help him; after that they would have little warning of the night. Later on, the meeting place was noted, such as a cross-roads or hillock, so that nobody knew until the last minute where the cottage was to be. The friends would assemble—each with his tool to do the particular work allotted to him. ... Their work would be begun as secretly as possible, about ten o'clock; sometimes there would be thirty to forty workers, according to the man's popularity,—some of them building, and others on the look-out in case anybody came to hinder them. Then, in the early hours of the morning the wife of the new house would bring up food for the workers before they dispersed, and they set about lighting a fire on the new hearth, for the house was regarded as being safe, according to the law and the sentiment of the land, when smoke arose from the chimney.

This happened usually in the summer, as early as possible, since there would be the second house to build before autumn, and when that had been finished, the cow as a rule would spend the winter in the first cottage, while the cottager and his family moved to the new house. During the winter and spring the cottager would clear his land of stones and dry it so as to ensure a little grain and potatoes. The way the farmers and landowners prevented this was to join together and set a date in the summer when it would be possible to make the greatest damage to the cottager's crops and hedges. A number of cottagers would be visited in one day, and rascals from afar—court bailiffs, drunken idlers from Lampeter, Aberystwyth and Tregaron. Amongst these would be lawyers, an occasional landowner and farmer and a policeman, who would form a circle around the cottager lest he break the law, as they used to say.

Cymru, 48 (1915), 205–7. (Translated)

a temporary arrangement built by the combined effort of from twenty to thirty people to meet the 'legal' requirement. The original turf building, put up usually in early summer, would be superseded by a second more permanent house before autumn, when the first building would be converted into a cowshed. The poet Thomas Edwards ('Twm o'r Nant') in a poem written about 1780 on behalf of a poor mole-catcher seeking help from his neighbours to build such a house on the mountain near Llanuwchllyn, Merioneth, calls on every one to give what he can—wood or money in particular—and, of course, his labour for a day or two. The carpenter, slater and blacksmith, he hopes, will listen to his plea, so that the mole-catcher, who, we are informed, is aged and infirm, will be able to build his house and enclose his plot. It is clear from other descriptions that the doors, windows and other fittings would be constructed beforehand, so that the actual work on the fateful night would consist of bringing them to the site ready for assembly, cutting the turf and building the walls and roof by dawn. The unenclosed waste lands on which many of these squatters' cottages were built were subsequently enclosed by Act of Parliament in the late eighteenth and early nineteenth centuries. It has been estimated that approximately one-fifth of the total area of Wales was in this way turned into private ownership during this period. Squatters who had occupied their houses for at least twenty years before the enclosure act was passed, were usually allowed to retain their cottages and land. In districts such as the Llŷn peninsula their haphazard field and settlement pattern still stands out in contrast to the surrounding geometrically-shaped holdings where the land was legally parcelled out.

Clubs

Apart from mutual aid in building the *tŷ unnos*, there are one or two other minor instances of the kind of co-operation which manifested itself above all in the formation of friendly societies. Book clubs, for example were founded in many Welsh towns, such as Cowbridge, Pembroke, Denbigh and Holyhead, as a reading public emerged. Sometimes a more sophisticated form of co-operation was promoted for purely commercial reasons by entrepreneurial craftsmen. The well-known clockmaker, Samuel Roberts of Llanfair Caereinion, Montgomeryshire, for example, established a clock club in the 1770s to promote the sale of his long-case clocks. The twenty members apparently met every month and paid a regular subscription of two shillings, each meeting raising a sum sufficient to buy a clock. The recipient of the clocks at each of these meetings was probably decided by lottery, and every member could be certain that he would receive his clock within two years. Such clubs were criticized, however, because poor people, who had been persuaded to join but had failed to keep up their regular payments, had been known to forfeit the contributions they had already made, as well as the clocks, which were confiscated. However, in an age of incipient commercialism, the clock clubs, as Dr W.T.R. Pryce suggests, reflected the same spirit and purpose as were to be found in the early building societies.

Social censure and the 'ceffyl pren'

It is important to remember that members of the traditional community came together not only in the various forms of mutual aid discussed above, but also to reflect popular opinion in such a way as to exercise unofficial social control over its wayward members, and sometimes to punish them. Such practices, which were to be found in many parts of Europe, went under a variety of names in Wales, *y ceffyl pren* (the wooden horse) being the best known; in the border counties the English terms 'riding the stang', 'skymmetry' and 'skimmington' were sometimes used, as well as *cwlstrin*, a form related, according to the University of Wales Dictionary, to the English 'to ride on a cowl-staff'. An effigy of a person who had contravened the moral code was carried on a wooden pole, or on a chair placed on a ladder, at the head of a procession which paraded outside his (or her) house to the accompaniment of 'rough music', namely the beating of saucepans and other utensils. The intention was to draw attention to the breach and to make a laughing stock of the miscreant. Marital strife and marriages where the couple were ill-matched in age were sufficient reason for the *ceffyl pren* procession to be staged. Marital infidelity might lead to more drastic treatment, the offending parties being fastened, back to back, and mounted on the wooden horse before being paraded and pelted with rotten eggs. A mock court might be held, as happened in Cynwyl Elfed, Carmarthenshire, in 1865, when a effigy was tried and subsequently burnt. A similar court, in the Vale of Glamorgan, described in detail by Charles Redwood in 1839, was held with great solemnity in a churchyard, the 'judge' being accompanied by attendant officers, bearing white wands, and mock advocates. The verdict of the trial was that the inhabitants should 'hold a riding' on the husband

64

and wife, the 'judge' and his entourage again participating in the procession in which, to the accompaniment of 'rough music', a petticoat and a pair of trousers were carried on separate poles, preceding a man and a woman impersonating the married couple. In Llanfyllin, Montgomeryshire, if a man and his wife quarrelled openly, the *ceffyl pren* was taken to their door and following dog-gerel, in the form of question and answer, recited,

'Am bwy 'r wyt ti' marchogaeth?'
'Am ddeuddyn o'r gymdogaeth.'
'Pwy yw'r rheiny, Gymro?'
'Wil ac Ali Beuno.'
'A ydyw Ali'n curo'n arw?'
'Mae hi bron a'i ladd e'n farw,
Rhwng y ferch a hithau
Mae'r gwr yn las o'i gleisiau!'

('For whom are you riding?' 'For two people from the neighbourhood.' 'Who are those, Welshman?' 'Wil and Ali Beuno.' 'Does Ali beat hard?' 'She has nearly killed him. Between the daughter and her, the husband is blue with bruises.')

When the community took the law into its own hands in this way the outcome was often unpredictable. In 1834, for example, the offender who was to be punished by the *ceffyl pren* in Llanba-darn Trefeglwys, Cardiganshire, was apprehended by the mob on returning home from an auction. He drew his knife in a vain attempt to resist, and was so severely beaten about the head in the ensuing affray that he died three hours later. As a means of social control, however, there can be no doubt that the *ceffyl pren* was generally effective. As an old woman, who was aged ninety-six in 1858 reported, she had often seen the *ceffyl pren* in Breconshire used 'with great effect, as quarrelsome women had a great dread of its appearance'.

The *ceffyl pren* treatment was also meted out in other examples of unapproved behaviour besides marital and sexual misconduct, such as when witnesses had given evidence in unpopular court cases. This happened frequently during the Rebecca Riots which flared up periodically between 1838 and 1843 in Dyfed. According to Professor David Williams, in his detailed study of the agrarian discontent of this period, 'it can, indeed, be said that the Rebecca Riots were an extension of the practice of the *ceffyl pren*'. Although the Riots, with their attacks on toll-gates by Rebecca and her 'Daughters'—men heavily disguised in women's clothes and with blackened faces—were for the most part confined to south-west Wales, the *ceffyl pren* was to be found in all parts of the country.

Industrial blacklegs and the Scotch Cattle

The 'Scotch Cattle' of the populous iron-working and coal-mining communities of the south-east in this period belonged to the same type of pre-industrial ritual although applied to new social circumstances. '"Scotching" was a means employed by the ignorant and dissatisfied workman to coerce his fellow-labourer and to prevent him working otherwise than according to the united decree, determined at meetings held for that purpose'. These meetings were held at night on the hill slopes and were attended by as many as a thousand colliers. The leader of the Scotch Cattle was *y Tarw Scotch*, the Scotch Bull; his unheeded warnings were followed by a 'midnight visit' by groups of from ten to twenty miners. According to D.J.V.Jones,

> The leaders of the party were disguised by masks, handkerchiefs, and cattle skins; the remainder had blackened faces, and wore women's clothes, 'their best clothes', or simply reversed jackets. They announced their arrival by blowing a horn, rattling chains, and making 'low' noises. At the home of their victim the Cattle smashed the windows with stones or pickaxes and broke down the door. Once inside, it was a relatively easy matter to destroy the furniture and earthenware, and to set fire to clothes and curtaining. The inhabitant might be ill-treated or given a further warning; then the Cattle disappeared as swiftly as they had arrived, leaving their glistening red mark on the open door.

Their victims, according to Dr Jones, were the uncommitted, the blackleg, and the strike-breaker.

Popular sports—football, 'cnapan', 'bando' and handball

The community spirit of the pre-industrial period revealed so clearly in mutual aid and social control also manifested itself in the various unofficial forms of recreation which were practised in the countryside. These were often associated with feast days, when the treadmill of labour was temporarily halted and young men were free to participate. Football was played until dark on Christmas Day in Dolgellau and Maentwrog, Merioneth. The hunting of rabbits and squirrels was also popular on this day, as well as fox-hunting on Boxing Day. Old New Year's Day, Shrove Tuesday and the patronal festivals were three other occasions when a rough variety of football, involving an unlimited number of players and few rules, was widely played, often between two neighbouring parishes, the respective churches, usually several miles apart, being the goals in each case. William Bulkeley of Brynddu, records in his diary several instances of such games in

Anglesey, including the annual derby which took place in 1741 on 15 March:

> This being the great football match day between Llanfechell and its associated parishes and Llanbadrick and its associated parishes, Llanfechell party were most shamefully beaten, as indeed they have been these three last years.

Although interparochial football matches were also to be found in Dyfed, it was here, where the three historical counties of Carmarthen, Cardigan and Pembroke meet that the game of *cnapan* was formerly played. The *cnapan* was the hard wooden ball, the size of a cricket ball, which was thrown into the air at the start of the game and then hit or carried and passed from player to player (among the 500 or 600 participants—some of them mounted on horseback) until the goal, some two miles away, was reached. *Cnapan*, which survived until the last century, was described by George Owen in 1590 when the matches took place on Shrove Tuesday, Easter Monday, the Saturday after Easter (*Pasg bach*), Ascension Day and *Gŵyl Corff Crist* (Corpus Christi). As in many early games, there seem to have been few rules, and injuries were rife.

Like *cnapan*, another well-known interparochial game, *bando*, was played with a wooden ball of the size of a cricket ball, but in this case a stick, not unlike a hockey stick, was used by the players. The game, which was particularly popular in Glamorgan in the first half of the nineteenth century, was played on an open space, the beaches at Cynffig (Kenfig) and Llantwit Major being the venues of two well-known contests between local teams of which descriptions have survived. According to Charles Redwood's account, the number of players was between twenty and thirty a side, and the pitch some 200 yards long; the games, we are told, drew a large number of spectators and supporters.

Glamorgan was well known in the last century for another sport which had earlier had a wider distribution. This was *chwarae pêl*, (lit. ball-playing) or handball, played originally against the church wall on Sundays, later against a blank wall of a house, but, in its most developed form, on a specially built three-walled court, not unlike a squash court without a rear wall. One such court still survives in Nelson, where it was formerly associated with a local hotel, and several other sites have been identified in the county. Handball, as played in Glamorgan, is said to have been identical to its namesake in Ireland and to have involved two

*The handball court at Nelson, Glamorgan, shown in this 1914 photograph,
is still in existence and in occasional use.*

or four players, each in turn striking the ball (about four inches
in diameter) with his hand, against the wall, until one of them
failed to return it, whereupon points were awarded to his oppo-
nent. The play area was marked and lined, but the size of the
courts, scoring methods and length of the games were never stan-
dardized, thus limiting the sport's expansion. 'Fives', which was
similar in origin, but with different rules and techniques, became
incorporated in England into the recreational activities of the public schools, and it was through this association that fives courts
came to be built in the nineteenth century in Welsh schools such
as those in Pengam, Cowbridge and Llandovery, as well as St
David's College, Lampeter.

The May celebrations

One of the most popular festivals of the year in Wales was the
celebration of *Calan Mai*, May Day, which marked the beginning
of the summer half of the year when traditionally the centre of
social life and work moved from the hearth to the open air. As
Alwyn and Brinley Rees said of the Celtic countries,'Summer is
the period when nature is awake, and when young people used
to leave the winter homestead to spend their time in their summer

May-dancing in Flintshire in the early nineteenth century

Some time in April (perhaps the *first* of April) ten, fifteen or twenty, more or less, of the young people of a parish or district settle to go about on the first of May to *dawnsio haf* [go summer-dancing], and then they get a seamstress in the neighbourhood to prepare for them a *cangen* [branch], as it is called, namely a piece of wood similar to the Merioneth straw-fork, or similar to the letter 'Y'. The preparation is as follows: they dress the two arms and the space between them with a strong cloth and cover it with a fine cloth and silks, and then they sew on it ornaments of various kinds, such as watches, from one to ten or more, silver dishes of different sizes and shapes, such as spoons, flesh-hooks and tea-pots, etc., and among them there will be bundles of silken ribbons, most frequently of a verdant colour. On the morning of May Day at dawn, these dancers assemble in their fancy dress ... To each *haf* [dancing group, lit. summer] there belongs a *crythwr* [crowder, fiddler], *ynfyd-ddyn* [fool], and *cadi* (as they are called in this district). But to say a word about the clothes of these people: all of these, except the last two named, appear in their own clothes, albeit their best clothes, but the *ynfyd-ddyn*, or the *ffŵl* [fool], as he is called, in clothes of various kinds, some shabby and some splendid; a monstrous veil [*gorchudd*] full of holes is placed over his soot-blackened face, and feathers in his hat, and a wooden sword in his hand; the *ynfyd-ddyn* is very accurately represented as regards attitude, dress and appearance. The *cadi*, as she is called, is in a woman's clothes, her clothes filthy and her behaviour discourteous; in one hand there is a ladle and in the other a besom.

After they have assembled and worn their decorations, they set out on their journey; and when they have come to a house the *crythwr* begins to play his tune and the *hafwyr* dance in front of the door; and as they dance they wave white handkerchiefs in their hands; they do this regularly and all at once. While they dance the *ynfyd-ddyn* and the *cadi* run to the house to request and receive the gifts of the occupants.

Y Gwyliedydd, 1823, 306–8. (Translated)

dwellings, tending their herds on the hills and indulging in outdoor pastimes. By November Eve (*Samain*), they returned again to the old home and spent the winter nights plying their fireside crafts, listening to fireside stories and entertaining themselves indoors'. Like November Eve, or Hallowe'en, both May Eve and St John's Eve at midsummer were occasions when divination was practised because of the proximity of the supernatural world to our own mundane existence at these turning-points in the yearly cycle. The lighting of bonfires on these three nights originated as a means of foretelling the future from the way in which the bones had burned in what were literally 'bone-fires'. It is interesting to reflect that, partly as a result of the confusion brought about by the change in the calendar in 1752, both the fire rites linked with the Winter's Eve celebrations, and those associated with Midsummer, had acquired a political connotation by the last century in Britain and North America. Guy Fawkes bonfires on the Fifth of November mark the treason of a man who was put to death by hanging, not, as one would suppose, by burning at the stake; and the Fourth of July firework displays commemorating the Independence Day of the former American colonies probably derive from the old Midsummer's Eve bonfires which continued to be held according to the old calendar. It is also significant, that whereas Winter's Eve and Midsummer's Eve were both taken over at an early date by the Christian Church as All Hallows and St John's Eve festivals respectively, May Day remained predominantly a secular, if not a pagan, feast, acquiring, like the other two feasts, a political significance in modern times as an international holiday marking the importance of labour. The only inroad which religion made upon the May Day tradition was the *canu haf* (summer singing) popularized in the seventeenth century when pious carols were sung outside the houses very early on May morning, the parties being rewarded in the wassailing tradition by being invited into the house and regaled with food and drink.

The maypole customs, which were considerably older in origin, were linked with the advent of a new season of plant growth and fertility, and with the decoration of houses with flowers in its honour. The birch tree, which symbolized summer, was associated with two festivals, namely, May Day and Midsummer, and took two forms, that of the maypole, *y fedwen haf* (summer birch) which was erected in a village on either or both of these festivals, and the *cangen haf* (summer branch) which was carried around from house to house, mainly on May Day. The former was more widely found in south Wales, where rivalry between villages led to the theft of the maypole—as happened frequently in the Vale of Glamorgan—and the latter was characteristic of north-east Wales. Both were associated with dancing, the former around the highly decorated raised pole, and the latter accompanying the summer branch decorated with watches and similar objects as it moved from house to house to the banter of the *Cadi ha'*, or Fool character, and his party of dancers with blackened faces.

May Day generally saw the beginning of a summer season of open-air activities, including those associated with the *twmpath chwarae* (lit. 'play mound'), which was formally opened with great ceremony in Llansanffraid-ym-Mechain, Montgomeryshire, on this day. On the mound would be seated the harper or fiddler who would be employed for the season to accompany the dancing which would be the main pastime during the long summer evenings, his remuneration being paid from a fund raised for the purpose. Games were also played, including tennis and bowling, throwing the stone and beam, and wrestling, 'under the supervision of some veteran as master of the ceremonies, all observing strictly the rules of the green'. The name *chwareufa gampau*, which was used in Merioneth, emphasizes the *campau* or feats which were performed at these places. The twenty-four feats (*y pedair camp ar hugain*) of Welsh tradition included, besides accomplishments in music, poetry and board games, ten manly feats—physical prowess, running, jumping, swimming, wrestling and riding, together with feats of arms, such as sword-play—and ten youthful feats including hunting birds, fishing, and hunting with a greyhound. Robert Thomas, 'Ap Fychan', who was born in 1809, in describing the feats of the menfolk of the Llanuwchllyn of his childhood, distinguishes between feats at work (including farm skills) and *campau difyrru* (feats of entertainment) which included 'throwing the stone and bar, kicking the ball, running and wrestling', suggesting that these physical accomplishments of the men of Merioneth had changed but little.

In Glamorgan the summer recreational meeting was the *taplas haf* (revels), which began on Easter Monday and was held every Saturday throughout the summer until All Hallows' Day. Two printed handbills have survived, which relate to the 'gambols',or sports, in this tradition, held over three days in June 1780, in Llangyfelach, near Swansea, consisting of races of all kinds, shooting at a mark, 'flinging the bar', bandy and football matches, as well as intriguing competitions such as 'old women's grinning match'.

Such 'gambols' were commercial operations arranged by innkeepers, who requested subscriptions towards the prizes. In many respects they were the forerunners of our modern village carnivals and sports.

4 Church Festivals and Practices

Celtic and medieval traditions

As part of medieval Christendom Wales shared fully in the 'Great Tradition' of western Europe which was mediated through the Church and its clergy. The 'Little Tradition', which, as Robert Redfield pointed out in his elaboration of these twin concepts, 'works itself out and keeps itself going in the lives of the unlettered in their village communities', retained many of the customs which had been nurtured in the Middle Ages, long after the unity of the Church and its domination of social life had been undermined by the forces of the Reformation. Many of the folk customs which drew the attention of the antiquaries of the eighteenth century and after were explained as 'popish ceremonies' which had outlived the religious system which had generated them. Although they had been shorn of their original meaning in the intervening process of social change, they still enlivened the everyday life of the communities which the early folklorists recorded.

The medieval church, in its turn, overlay a much earlier Celtic tradition which dated from the fifth century. Although Christianity may have been introduced during the Roman occupation and survived marginally, the formative period in the establishment of Christianity as the dominant religion occurred in the 'Age of the Saints' when the ideas and doctrines were re-introduced. These re-entered Britain from the west along the seaways which had maintained contact with what had remained of Roman civilization in Gaul and the western Mediterranean. E.G. Bowen has argued that the Celtic saints who disseminated the new religion were not necessarily missionaries to the people at large and that the churches which they established were not intended for congregational worship. The object of their zeal was the conversion of the local chieftains and their families, resulting in the erection of small churches on their land. Many of these cells were established away from the existing centres of population in clearings which in time might acquire their own settlements of farms and houses. Some of the 'mother churches' which were in effect quite large monastic settlements, were, in contrast, located nearer the areas of contemporary settlement on the periphery of the central highland area of Wales. On the whole, however, these new, small internal colonies were situated lower down the slopes than the hill-forts on the uplands, in or near which the native population had lived immediately prior to the Roman occupation. 'The majority of settlements established by the saints in Wales', concludes E.G. Bowen, 'are in lowlying parts of the country, on the lower valley-slopes and on the valley-floors, and especially in close proximity to the sea and to tidal waters'.

The naming of the 'llan'

The *llan* (pl. *llannau*), or enclosure, associated with these early religious settlements contained a church dedicated to a Celtic saint who is usually assumed to have been its founder. It has been pointed out, however, that it is not possible, in the absence of surviving evidence, to verify the direct association between a saint and the churches dedicated to him. According to Dr Wendy Davies, 'the likelihood is that only a very small proportion of dedications represents foundations directly associated with the saint'. Subsequent re-dedications and possible revivals in the popularity of the cults of various saints during the medieval period have undoubtedly clouded the issue; nevertheless the extent of these early settlements and their influence on the subsequent development of Wales cannot be gainsaid. E. G. Bowen has identified over 600 dedications to Celtic saints in various parts of Wales and some in the neighbouring parts of England. This figure excludes many which were lost when churches, as so often happened, were re-dedicated to Mary and Michael in the eleventh and twelfth centuries.

Scattered settlement patterns

In his analysis of the 614 known Celtic dedications E.G. Bowen examines the subsequent settlements which have emerged around these early sites and finds that 268, or forty-four per cent, are either isolated churches or minute nucleations restricted to a vicarage or rectory with possibly a single farm alongside. Although this computation is based on the modern settlement pattern, it is borne out by such historical evidence as exists in the nineteenth-century Tithe Maps and the first edition of the Ordnance Survey, as well as the incomplete information on the subject collected by Edward Lhuyd at the end of the seventeenth century in his parochial queries. A further 135, or twenty-two per cent, of these settlements comprised only a handful of houses, while there were only fifty-five, or nine per cent, which could be described as 'church villages' having as many as thirty to forty houses clustered around the church. The remainder of the settlements (156 or twenty per cent) had for the most part developed from the other categories under the influence of urban tendencies during the Anglo-Norman period, and in subsequent centuries as a result of industrialization. The outstanding characteristic of the settlement pattern which developed on these early sites, according to E.G. Bowen, 'is the fact that over much of Wales the Celtic saints established many more potential nuclei of settlement than the cultural and economic life of the community has been able to develop in subsequent times'.

Apart from the incorporation of some of these early settlements in the urban centres established by the Anglo-Normans, or their replacement by the new boroughs, the medieval period saw the introduction of a parochial system on the continental pattern to replace the haphazard territorial organization of the earlier Celtic church. Parishes were carved out gradually in the twelfth and thirteenth centuries and became the basis for the collection of tithes for the maintenance of the churches and their clergy. In the moorland districts these new geographical units, which were subsequently to replace the medieval townships of pre-Conquest origin as the major local territorial unit, often comprised sparsely populated communities and extensive tracts of uncultivated land. In those areas of early Norman settlement, in contrast, the knight's fee, as in the Vale of Glamorgan, often became the unit on which the new ecclesiastical unit was based. Whatever their geographical extent and the details of their origin, church and parish in the medieval period became the basis of a form of social organization which Wales shared with much of the rest of Europe, even though it was far less nucleated, urbanized and centralized in the settlement pattern to which it gave rise. Even the four Welsh cathedral cities which might have been expected to acquire urban characteristics were hardly larger than villages.

Religious sites and continuity with the past

The parish church around which this social and cultural life revolved was a building intended from the very beginning for the performance of religious rites. Usually aligned from east to west, with the altar to the east, the church and its surrounding churchyard were usually enclosed by a stone wall marking out the *llan* in the original meaning of that word. In some cases, notably the well-known circular churchyard at Ysbyty Cynfyn in Cardiganshire, the enclosure is earlier than the church itself. Moreover, many churches, such as those at Llanwrthwl, Breconshire, and Maentwrog, Merioneth, are clearly located near prehistoric monuments, suggesting a cultural continuity with pre-Christian sacred sites. Traditions associated with many churches, such as Llanfihangel Genau'r Glyn, Cardiganshire, Llanbryn-mair, Llanfyllin and Meifod, Montgomeryshire, and Corwen, Merioneth, refer to repeated unsuccessful attempts to erect the original building on a site other than the present one, each day's labour being undone overnight by supernatural forces until the work was finally abandoned in favour of what had obviously been intended to be the chosen site. By the time of the Reformation the diminutive churches of Celtic origin had been replaced by (or incorporated in) more substantial buildings in one or other of the medieval architectural styles.

Veneration of Celtic relics

Vestiges of the widespread devotion to the Celtic saints were preserved in many of these churches, alongside medieval Catholic relics, as objects of pilgrimage and veneration, and their efficacy in the working of cures and charms often believed in as late as the nineteenth century. In St David's Cathedral a shrine to the patron saint was built *c*.1275 to display the relics more prominently, and even in some of the smaller churches the memory of lesser saints was kept alive for many centuries by the preservation of objects associated with their cults. At Llandderfel, Merioneth, *Ceffyl Derfel* (Derfel's Horse), a wooden image of a man on horseback, was venerated as a relic of the sixth-century saint to whose church cattle and horses were brought to be cured and blessed. The image, which also possessed striking powers to protect men from disaster and to rescue their souls from purgatory, was visited by hundreds daily at the time of the Reformation. It (or its successor) was kept near the communion table until 1730 and taken out every Easter Tuesday to be ridden by children. It was subsequently decapitated and kept in the church porch together with a staff (*ffon Dderfel*) said to have belonged to the saint. Similarly, St Beuno was commemorated at his shrine in Clynnog, Caernarfonshire, as late as the nineteenth century, by offerings of money placed in his chest (*cyff Beuno*) in the parish church on his feast day, 21 April, for the prosperity of the cattle; lambs and calves bearing his mark (*nod Beuno*) were sold to raise the money for this purpose. In Beuno's chapel, too, 'his votaries afflicted by any malady were laid for the night, with a full confidence of receiving a cure'.

Holy wells

The healing powers of the Celtic saints were associated not only with the churches dedicated to them but also with the numerous wells bearing their names and undoubtedly dating back to early Christian, if not pre-Christian times. Many of these ancient sites had later superstructures or stone walls encasing the well itself. One of the most famous was St Winifred's Well (*Ffynnon Gwenfrewi*) at Holywell, Flintshire, which marked the site of the martyrdom and subsequent miraculous restoration to life of the seventh-century saint. The popularity of this well survived the Reformation and continues to the present day. Other wells were more modest in scale. Ffynnon Gybi, Llangybi, Caernarfonshire, nevertheless

St Dwynwen's Well, Anglesey, in 1807

The place was much resorted to formerly and continued in repute to our days. There was a spring of clear Water, now choaked up by the sands, at which an old woman from Niwbwrch [Newborough] always attended and prognosticated the lover's success from the movement of some small eels which waved out of the sides of the well, on spreading the suitor's handkerchief on the surface of the water. I remember an old woman saying that when she was a girl, she consulted the woman of this well about her destiny with respect to the husband. On spreading her handkerchief, out popped an eel from the North side of the well; and soon after another crawled from the south side, and they both met on the bottom of the well: then the woman told her that her husband wod [sic] be a stranger from the south part of Caernarvonshire. Sometime after it happened that three brothers came from that part and settled in the neighbourhood where the young woman was; one of whom made his addresses to her, and in a little time married her. This is the substance of the story as far as I remember it. These [sic] couple were my father and mother.

William Williams, Llandygai. National Library of Wales MS 822, p. 5–7.

Bathers at St Winifred's Well, Holywell, Flintshire, c. 1890.

had two elaborate well-chambers built in the eighteenth century when the medicinal qualities of the water were found to be 'of much efficacy in scrofulous cases'. Yet others, certainly the most numerous category, while retaining a nominal association with an early saint (or with the Virgin Mary), fell into disuse in the nineteenth century, having served as wishing wells, their religious origin all but forgotten.

Churchyard practices and burial

Practices and beliefs associated with the use of the churchyard and the church itself, were recorded by antiquarians and folklorists in the eighteenth and nineteenth centuries, particularly clergymen, who were not only interested in ecclesiastical history but were well placed to gather such information. The Revd Elias Owen (1833–99), who was one of the most prominent and reliable of these clerics, became the diocesan examiner in scriptural know-ledge in the church schools of the See of St Asaph in 1876 and in the course of his journeys throughout the diocese was able to collect a considerable amount of information about church traditions in the Vale of Clwyd and the vicinity, where he later settled as parish priest. He confirms, for example, that the northern side of the churchyard was unused for burials in many parishes (except for suicides, unbaptized infants and executed persons) until the eighteenth century or even later. In many Montgomeryshire churches the absence of graves in the north side of the churchyard and of early windows in the north wall of the church was still noticeable and was linked to the use of that part of the churchyard for popular sports such as ball-playing and cock-fighting (as in Llanfechain, Montgomeryshire). Handball was played against the church walls on a Sunday until the bells ceased pealing, whereupon both players and spectators in a body entered the church for the service. This practice had ceased in Clocaenog, Denbighshire, in the 1820s. However, in Betws-y-coed and Llanbedr-y-cennin, Caernarfonshire, the scoring marks of the ball game are still to be seen scratched on the church wall. Such lamentable behaviour lay behind the complaint by an earlier antiquary, Archdeacon Henry Thomas Payne (1759–1832) in 1785 about the churchyard in Llangatwg, Breconshire, especially the 'licentiousness of young people in their amusements there on Sunday evenings and on other occasions'. Cwm-du in the same county, he notes, was 'like many (indeed most) other churchyards in this part of Wales, much trodden down and disfigured by the idle Diversions of young people who ought to be restrained'. Dancing in the churchyard, according to another writer, was common in many areas: 'their churchyards serve the Dead for a Burying and the Living for a Dancing-place, and that every Sunday; for there you shall see a blind Harper mounted upon a Grave stone, making admirable Harmony and surrounded by the hang-eared Tribe, like another Orpheus amongst the Beasts'.

The use of the north of the churchyard for burials was, on the whole, a relatively recent development. In Llansanffraid-ym-Mechain, Montgomeryshire, the vicar told Elias Owen that his predecessor, who died in 1846, was the first to be buried in the north part of the churchyard (which was nearly full when he wrote in 1886). Archdeacon Payne, writing about Breconshire, suggests that burial in any part of the churchyard had been rather uncommon in some districts in that county, 'the pride of the country people in burying their dead within the churches', resulting in the dilapidation of their structure, graves being dug very near the foundations thus endangering the fabric. Because of the frequency of burials in the 1780s the graves, he tells us, were overfilled with scarcely enough earth to cover the dead. A serious complaint

Caernarfonshire burial customs c. 1800

When the parish bell announces the death of a person, it is immediately inquired upon what day the funeral is to be; and the night preceding that day all the neighbours assemble at the Tŷ Corph, i.e. the corpse's house. The coffin, with the remains of the deceased is then placed on stools in an open part of the house, covered with a black cloth, or if the deceased was unmarried, with a clean white sheet, with three candles burning on it. Every person on entering the house falls devoutly on his knee before the corpse, and repeats to himself the Lord's prayer, or another prayer that he chooses. Afterwards if he is a smoker, a pipe and tobacco are offered to him. This meeting is called *Gwylnos*, and in some places *pydreua*. The first word means vigil; the other is, no doubt, a common word from *paderau* or *padereuau*, that is, paters or paternosters. When the assembly is full, the parish clerk reads the common service appointed for the burial of the dead, at the conclusion of which psalms, hymns and other godly songs are sung, and since Methodism has become so universal, some one stands up and delivers an oration on the melancholy subject, and then the company drop away by degrees. On the following day ... all the neighbours assemble again. It is not uncommon to see on such occasions between three or four hundred persons or even more. These persons are then treated with warm spiced ale, cakes, pipes, and tobacco, and a dinner is given to all those that have come from afar. They then proceed to the church, and at the end of that part of the burial which is usually read in church, before the corpse is taken from the church. Every one of the congregation presents the officiating clergyman with a piece of money, the deceased's next relatives usually drop a shilling each, others sixpence, and the poorer sort a penny, laying it on the altar. This is called the offering, and the sum amounts sometimes to eight, ten or more pounds at a burial. The parish clerk has also his offering at the grave which amounts commonly to about one-fourth of what the clergyman receives.

William Williams, *Observations on the Snowdon Mountains*, 1802, 13–4.

had been made to him by the curate of Llanfeugan 'who declared he had oftentimes been obliged to quit the church, in the midst of divine service, being quite overcome with the stench from putrid carcases'. He cites the case of the Revd Mr Skinner who left instructions for his burial in the churchyard to set an example to his parishioners, and whose tombstone bore the Welsh inscription 'Yr eglwys i'r bobl, y fynwent i'r meirw' (The church for the people, the churchyard for the dead).

Tending the graves

In the churchyard itself the use of gravestones as permanent memorials dates from relatively recent times. In the course of an extensive modern survey carried out in Cardiganshire, it was discovered that of some tens of thousands of gravestones in the county dating from before 1900, the earliest surviving outdoor examples were those from the first decade of the eighteenth century. Travellers through Wales during this century refer to less permanent methods of marking out the burial places. In Caernarfon, all the graves (apart from tombs) were 'guarded by basketting of wickerwork, and stuck with evergreens'. In another part of north Wales, the graves of departed friends were said to be planted with various evergreens, 'box, thrift and other plants fit for edging and planted round in the shape of the grave for a border, and every flower that adorns the smart parterre is placed within'. The choice was apparently determined by the age of the deceased; snowdrop, violet, primrose ('harbingers of spring') were for the young; rocket, rose, woodbine for those of maturer years; and tansy, rue and starwort for those in declining life. They were said to be constantly weeded, usually on a Saturday afternoon. An inner enclosure within an outer enclosure on a grave usually denoted a young child and its mother who had died in childbirth. In the Mold district of Flintshire, green leaves, such as rushes, flags and branches of box, as well as flowers, were used to decorate the graves throughout the year following the burials, after which they would be covered by stones.

The Cardiganshire survey suggests that tombstones were quite often not erected for a considerable time after the burial, and the practice noted in Mold no doubt represented an intermediate stage. Erasmus Saunders, describing conditions in the diocese of St David's in 1721, refers to the practice 'in mountainous parts' of kneeling and praying near the graves of friends, especially at Christmas, at cock-crowing, bringing a candle and torch and singing *halsingod* (religious songs). The reference is not so much to grave decoration with lighted candles, as is still to be found on the continent on All Souls' Eve, as to commemoration before the early-morning *plygain* service to which lighted candles were brought in many parts of Wales. J.T.Barber, visiting Briton Ferry in 1803, while noting the custom of planting evergreens on the graves of departed friends, also remarks that they were bedecked with flowers at certain seasons of the year, probably Christmas, Easter and Whitsun, as Iolo Morganwg records in his list of Glamorgan customs. It is probably from this latter practice that the widespread decoration of graves with flowers on Palm Sunday (which was also known as 'Flowering Sunday' or *Sul y Blodau*) developed later in the nineteenth century, especially in the industrial towns of south Wales. Palm Sunday, incidentally, was also an occasion for the decoration of the interior of the church, as occurred in Llanasa, Flintshire, where willow branches were draped on the pulpit.

Supernatural powers

Many old churches in Denbighshire and Flintshire (e.g. Rhuddlan, Clocaenog, Llannefydd, Gwaunysgor and Gwyddelwern), Elias Owen had observed, had originally had a door in the north wall which had subsequently been blocked. The practice, which had been recorded at Kerry, Montgomeryshire, had been to open the door during a baptism service, just as the clergyman entered the church, so that the Evil One could escape. The baptismal font and the stoup containing holy water, which gave supernatural protection, were located near the south door of the church. The entire building at times possessed a peculiar potency. To look through the keyhole of the church door at midnight on All Hallows Eve, for example, having first recited the Lord's Prayer backwards and walked around the church a requisite number of times, was to acquire the power to see the apparitions of those who were destined to die during the following year. The earth from the traditional unpaved floor of the church, mingled as it was with the remains of the dead, was also potent, and in Dolwyddelan, Caernarfonshire, in the eighteenth century, it was customary to use this soil in the preparation of an ointment to cure rashes and sores which was said to be very effective. Such earthen floors were usually strewn with rushes, partly to fill up the inequalities resulting from the frequent interments, and partly for warmth and comfort when the congregation kneeled. A traveller visiting Maentwrog church, Merioneth, in 1796, described it as a miserable place and noted that 'they put hay below the seats to kneel upon, which has a dirty appearance'. Elias Owen records the practice as still surviving in Gyffylliog, Denbighshire, and Gwaunysgor, Flintshire, in the first half of the nineteenth century. The churches were usually cleared out at certain seasons—Easter being one— when fresh rushes replaced the old ones.

Social hierarchy

The installation of pews was a relatively late feature in the development of the parish church, and their location within the building reflected the status of their occupants, hence the frequent disputes which occurred in the sixteenth and seventeenth centuries between rival claimants. In a well-documented case from Llandygai, Caernarfonshire, in 1575, the plaintiff, Sir Rees Griffith of Penrhyn, successfully argued that the defendants, William Griffith ap Llewelyn ap Grono and his son John, had no right to sit and kneel at the bench along the south side of the chancel in the parish church, where, according to the depositions of several witnesses of advanced age, Sir Rees's father and mother and their 'train' had always had the right to worship. The Penrhyn family, which had its own chapel in the mansion, as well as chaplains to conduct their services at home, frequented the parish church only on the four principal feasts of the year, whereupon all who were in the chancel departed to the body of the church to make way for them when they entered. The 'train' included important guests as well as children, servants and nurses. The defendants in the case were the son and grandson, respectively, of Sabel, who had nursed the plaintiff as a child, and who used to kneel 'in the nether end' of the chancel side, together with other nurses of the family during the services. When the family was absent, however, many other parishioners besides Sabel used to kneel there, suggesting that she had no special privilege other than as a member of the 'train'. The dispute had arisen because the defendants, knowing that Sir Rees Griffith's wife and her 'train' were attending church on a particular Sunday, had 'in very dispytefull maner' knelt beside her in the seat, and, when she had left her seat and 'repayred into the bodye of the sayd Church to here a Sermon ther made the sayd daye', had spitefully snatched her cushion, gloves and handkerchief and thrown them from the seat which they had continued to occupy. The reference to leaving the seat in order to be able to hear the sermon is an interesting reflection on contemporary practice, as is the evidence given by the witnesses concerning the right of Sir Rees Griffith's father to decide where inside the church the parishioners (who were all tenants of his) should be buried. He usually granted permission to bury his tenants, 'ffosters' and friends in the chancel, and had even allowed Sabel to be buried there 'in the sayd Seate'. Sir Rees, however, who was 'of greate worshipp & calling', was not so well disposed towards his old nurse Sabel's son and grandson, who are described as 'troblesome poore men & not meete to be Puefellowes in one Pue or seate wth the sayd plaintiff his wief, Children, or famelye'. Needless to say, he won his case.

The dominance of the landlord is also to be seen in the following century when the tenants of a single estate might be seated together in one part of the parish church. This is what happened in Llanfor, Merioneth, where a small chapel had been built on the north-east side of the chancel by the Price family of Rhiwlas to accommodate their tenants.

The order of leaving

The manner of leaving the church at the end of the service reflected the hierarchical structure of the congregation. Once the clergyman, who left first, had reached the porch, 'the gentlefolk left their seats and in the porch they exchanged courtesies with the parson. After a sufficient time had elapsed for these greetings to take place, other portions of the congregation departed; these again were succeeded by others, each portion taking precedence of others below them in the social scale, until all had left'. Elias Owen, who records this practice, mentions the rivalry which arose over the matter of precedence between the leading families of Llanfor. The building of the chapel by the Price family of Rhiwlas, according to a tradition he had heard, was the direct result of a dispute with the neighbouring Rhiwedog family as to who should leave the church first. After much unpleasantness, the matter had been referred to arbitrators who had decided in favour of the Rhiwedog claimants. The new chapel (Yr Eglwys Groes), which had been built in 1599, had its own door opening into the churchyard, thus enabling the Price family to escape humiliation when leaving the church.

The elaborate funerals of the gentry

It was, however, during the carefully organized funerals of the gentry in the parish churches that the status of the participants was most clearly to be seen. The arrangements on these occasions were often in the hands of experienced heralds who were careful to place the mourners in strict order of precedence both inside the church and in the funeral procession. When Sir Roger Mostyn was buried in 1642, the cortège was led by eighty-two poor persons dressed in white cloth, one for each year of the deceased's age, followed by gentry from all parts of north Wales and his heraldic

Funeral procession in the Trelech district of Carmarthenshire at the beginning of the twentieth century.

86

emblems. The undertaker (to use the modern term) was the herald Randal Holmes of Chester. Such elaborate funeral processions continued to be a feature of Welsh life until the end of the nineteenth century and later. That of the Revd John Elias the leading Methodist preacher of his day, who died in 1841, for example, naturally included numerous clergymen, many of them on horseback, as well as over forty carriages, and was estimated to be about a mile and a half in length and to include at least 10,000 people by the time it had reached Llangoed, Anglesey, where he was buried. The funeral of a leading landowner during the same century might be more structured although attended by fewer persons. When the Earl of Powis was buried in 1891, the hearse was preceded by 192 clergymen, ministers, mayors, councillors and major tenants—only those paying more than £200 in rent, numbering fifty-two, had been invited. Following these, who walked mostly in twos, were five carriages containing doctors, bishops, bearers, steward and valet. Then came twelve more bearers. After the hearse came forty-eight mourners in fourteen carriages, followed by the servants and estate employees, over forty Welshpool shopkeepers (by invitation), and 200 estate labourers, all walking in twos. These were followed by seventeen private carriages. In all, over 600 mourners took part in the procession to the church in Welshpool, in addition to those who lined the route.

Segregation of the sexes

Elias Owen also describes another arrangement which was sometimes to be found in the church during the services, namely the segregation of the sexes. This prevailed in the Jesus Chapel in Llanfair Dyffryn Clwyd which was built in 1623. A transept of Llangelynin Old Church, Caernarfonshire, he also tells us, was called *Capel Meibion* (the men's chapel) suggesting a similar arrangement. H.L. North records that the practice survived during funerals until the beginning of the present century in the churches of Caerhun and Llanllechid, Caernarfonshire. A similar arrangement existed in Pen-y-bryn Church, Cardiganshire, where the men sat on the north side and the women on the south side.

The role of the sexton

During the church service itself, a certain amount of authority might be exercised by the sexton, as in Kerry, Montgomeryshire, where he was said to perambulate the church during divine service wielding a bell to awaken drowsy listeners. No doubt it was he, too, who used the extending iron dog-tongs (*gefail gŵn*) which Elias Owen tells us were formerly to be found in every church in the Vale of Clwyd, and of which an example, dated 1815, is still to be seen in the church at Clynnog, Caernarfonshire. The sexton, in fact, was an important personage who was much closer to the parishioners than the incumbent, and who often provided a strong element of continuity and conservatism in parish life. The sextons of Llanllechid, Caernarfonshire, were drawn from among the members of a single family for over two hundred years. In another part of the county, William Roberts, sexton of Llannor, in 1745, wrote a scurrilous dramatic interlude attacking the Methodists who had recently begun to preach in the district much to the annoyance of Chancellor John Owen, his priest and master. Some sextons, like Dafydd Jones (1708?–85) of Trefriw, Caernarfonshire, Elis Roberts ('Elis y Cowper' d. 1789) of Llanddoged, Denbighshire, and Robert Ellis (1805–72) of Llanllyfni, Caernarfonshire, were minor literary figures who contributed to the local bardic tradition, including the composition of carols to be sung in the church in the early-morning *plygain* service on Christmas Day. This was the descendant of the midnight mass of the medieval Church which had become an abbreviated form of morning service beginning at six o'clock, or even earlier, followed by the singing of carols (often written especially for the occasion). The service continued until daylight, several parties taking part in turn before a packed and sometimes restless congregation. It was the sexton, too, who led the congregation in their responses during the Sunday services, and served as bell-ringer and grave-digger for the parish. He was remunerated for his duties by a dole of wheat, barley or oats referred to as *ŷd y gloch* or *ysgub y gloch* ('bell corn' or 'bell sheaf'). This was collected from all farmers until the passing of the Tithe Commutation Act of 1836 when the parish vestry made alternative arrangements to pay an annual sum equivalent to the value of the corn formerly received as *ŷd y gloch*. The sexton in many parts of north Wales also received *arian rhaw* ('spade money') at a funeral for his work as grave-digger. This was generally collected in the churchyard, the money being placed on the spade held out by the sexton for the purpose. This contribution was quite separate from the *offrwm* (offering) made in the church during the service when the congregation went forward individually, led by the nearest relatives of the deceased, to place their donations, usually a silver piece, on a small board attached to the altar rail. The rest of the congregation, first men, then women, filed up and gave smaller sums, usually a penny, the total later being announced by the clergyman. The origin of the offering was probably the pre-Reformation practice of paying the priest to say masses for the dead. This had become a personal gift to the officiating clergyman after the Reformation and could be used, if he so desired, to alleviate any hardship in the bereaved family. The offering was generally much greater in amount than the sum received by the sexton in the churchyard, and usually depended on the respectability of the deceased.

Bell-ringing

The other important duty of the sexton was bell-ringing. The passing bell, known as *cloch ened* in Dyfed, was rung to announce the death. This took place in the evening of the day on which the death had occurred, and not as the soul was departing.

> By varying the number of pulls the parishioners know whose passing bell is being rung: four pulls, thrice repeated with a pause between each set of pulls signifies a girl-child is dead, that is, the bell is tolled twelve times for a girl. Five pulls three times repeated, with a pause after each fifth, signifies the death of a boy-child; and six, seven, eight and nine pulls, three times repeated imply, respectively, that a single woman, an unmarried man, a married woman or a married man has departed this life.

This complicated system was still in use in Efenechtyd, where Elias Owen was the parish priest, but was not universally observed. In Llanfair, nearby, the pulls were not repeated three times, and a handbell was rung during funerals, the parish clerk walking a short distance in advance of the procession, thus ensuring that the road could be cleared of any approaching vehicle or obstacle. In other parishes the church bell was also rung after a funeral, sometimes, as in Llanasa and Caerwys, Flintshire, as soon as the grave was filled in. T. C. Evans, 'Cadrawd', (1846–1918), the historian of Llangynwyd, Glamorgan, states that the sexton in that parish was paid a shilling for ringing the passing bell, and when a person of higher status than usual was buried the bell was muffled on the day of the funeral from eight o'clock in the morning until the corpse arrived at the church. This was known as *mwrno'r gloch* (mourning the bell), and was done by tying an old felt hat around the tongue of the bell, the ringer waiting until the muffled sound had ceased before repeating the toll. For this the sexton was paid one pound. Llangynwyd church had six bells, and these were all rung during a wedding, beginning when the newly-married couple left the altar and set out from the church, and continuing intermittently throughout the day. The purpose was, of course, to announce that the wedding had taken place. In Caernarfonshire and Anglesey, the same purpose had given rise to the custom of holding a race from the church to the bride's house. The race began the moment the bride had worn her ring, and the wedding cake was the prize awarded to the fastest runner, as we saw in Chapter 3.

As in England, bell jingles were associated with various churches, for example, 'Tatw a sgadan, medd clychau Llanbadarn' (Potatoes and herring, say the bells of Llanbadarn). Other examples were recorded in Llangurig, Llandinam, Montgomery, Welshpool and Newtown. Curfew bells were rung at eight or nine o'clock in Caernarfon, Chirk and Dolgellau, and in the last-mentioned town *Y Gloch Goll* (the missing bell) was tolled when persons were missing on Cadair Idris.

Patronal festivals

One tradition which Wales shared with the rest of Europe was the patronal festival, or *gwylmabsant*, held on the feast day of the saint to whom the parish church was dedicated. For many centuries this was one of the most important events in the calendar of the local community, its origin probably being the pre-Christian celebrations in honour of local deities who were later superseded by Christian saints and martyrs. The well-known exhortation by Pope Gregory in AD 601 to St Augustine—that he should break not the temples of the idols but the idols—signified the beginning of the long process of adaptation which was to be the strategy of the Church throughout the medieval period in the conversion of Britain. The old celebrations should be changed to a better purpose. 'It may therefore be permitted them, that in the dedication days or other solemn days of martyrs, they make to them bowers about their churches, and feasting together after a good religious sort, kill their oxen now to the refreshing of themselves, to the praise of God, and increase of charity, which before they were wont to offer up in sacrifice to the devils'. The local festivals in Wales, as opposed to the great festivals of the Christian church, were first recorded in the eleventh century. They continued as social as well as religious festivals through the Middle Ages, surviving the upheaval of the Reformation, when an unsuccessful

The Wake at Holyhead from Edward Pugh's Cambria Depicta, *1816.*

attempt was made in 1536 to move the celebration of all dedications henceforth to the first Sunday in October. By the eighteenth and early nineteenth centuries, sapped by the attacks and rival attractions of Methodism, and having become mere shadows of their former selves, they finally petered out.

During the latter part of their long history the patronal festivals were recorded by diarists as part of the fabric of their everyday life, and in retrospect by antiquarians like Elias Owen who preserved the glowing memories of those old people who could recall the dying days of the *gwylmabsant* in their parishes. Religious writers during the same period, who saw in their disappearance the triumph of a superior life-style, also contributed their jaundiced evidence to the historical record. William Bulkeley, Brynddu, Llanfechell, an Anglesey gentleman, in his diary for 1749, refers to the wakes at Llanrhyddlad nearby, in early September, as did his namesake, the diarist from Dronwy, Llanfachraeth, 115 years earlier, in 1634. Both entries are for a Sunday which was the main day of the festival, the church service usually attracting a large congregation, including the inhabitants of neighbouring parishes. Football contests between the parishes, often

91

ending in physical violence, were a traditional feature of the *gwyl-mabsant* in Anglesey, as elsewhere, but the evidence of the Brynddu diarist suggests that these were declining in importance in the middle of the eighteenth century. The entertainment during the evening on these occasions included singing to the accompaniment of the harp, which continued until well into the night. A conscious attempt had been made in Holyhead in the 1740s to purge the local wakes of superstitious elements. The bones of the saint were previously carried through the town during the three Sundays of the three-week period of the wakes which were known as *Suliau'r Creiriau* (the Sundays of the Relics), and the celebrations were accompanied by feats of carrying water in the mouth and gravel in the hand from a well in the parish to the chapel of the saint as a form of marriage divination. Later evidence suggests that sports, including boat-races and horse-races, took the place of the older semi-superstitious observances in Holyhead. At Llan-badrig, nearby, a fair had replaced the football game, but during the Llaneilian wake, in the same district, the practice of divination flourished during the middle of the century; people entered a small semi-circular cupboard in a chapel adjacent to the church, and having turned around three times inside it, ensured that they would live out the year.

The *gwylmabsant* recalled by Elias Owen's informants in Den-bighshire during the second half of the following century, when it had become a thing of the past, included much that seemed to him to be innocent and pleasurable. People returned home for the wakes and renewed old acquaintances as well as cementing friendships. 'Boys and girls who had gone to service once more visited home and recounted to willing ears their joys and troubles. They, in return, received the history of the parish'. In his own parish of Efenechtyd, the wakes began on the Sunday before the feast of St Michael (the patron saint) and lasted until the Friday evening. 'Dancing, singing with the harp, trials of strength and agility and other manly sports, filled the hours of the afternoon, and, it is said, extended into the small hours of the night', with the attendant drinking to excess and fighting. In Efenechtyd the name for the Michaelmas Daisy was *Blodau Gwylmabsant 'Nech-tyd*.

It was customary for every one to wear a bunch of these flowers during the feast, and strangers begged them of the cottagers, who willingly gave a sprig, for they had taken care to cultivate the plant for this special purpose'. People would remark, 'The wakes are approaching, for the saints' flowers begin to blossom', and events in the traditional yearly round were linked with the occasion: the first goose was killed during this week, and the potato harvest began on the Wednesday during the wakes.

Parochial events were remembered by their having occurred so many weeks or months before or after the *gwylmabsant*, but, he lamented, 'the rising generation in this parish do not even know when the wakes were observed, and when the old people are gone the remembrance of the once celebrated festival will have disappeared'. In Efenechtyd, as well as in other parts of Wales, the celebration of the wakes had ceased during the 1840s largely because of the brutal fights associated with them. It had been this unruly element which had struck an earlier observer who thought that wakes in north Wales had, 'for ages past', lost every trait of religion. However, they were not carried on with one quarter of the spirit which influenced those who attended them thirty years previously, in the 1780s, when he could recollect such scenes of barbarity and disgrace in the Rhuthun district as would shame the people of his day.

The young men of the surrounding parishes would assemble all their force and visit the wake; and towards the evening, when the liquours had begun to operate upon their senses, the men of one parish would easily be provoked to quarrel with those of another, and both would turn out, and the encounter would commence with clubs, sticks and stones, in a most furious manner; the parties would break each other's lines, and then would ensue a desperate confusion. I have even seen females enter the list in defence of their brothers, and even in the middle of rivers, scuffle and contend with robust men.

Elias Owen's informants, for the most part, remembered a more tranquil patronal festival.

The gwylmabsant traditions of dancing and feasting
In other parts of Wales, dancing seems to have been a more prominent feature of the wakes. In Llanafan, Breconshire, there were still people alive in 1877 who remembered the lads and lasses of the surrounding district paying 5*s.* a quarter for dancing lessons

in preparation for the patronal festival which was held around All Hallows tide. A century earlier, in 1746, a traveller noted that dancing took place in the churchyard during the wakes at Diserth in the neighbouring county of Radnor: 'On one side of the church were about six couple dancing to one violin, and just below three or four couple to three violins, whose seat was a tombstone'. Elsewhere, as in Llanarmon-yn-Iâl, Denbighshire, the wakes at the beginning of the nineteenth century had had an emphasis on food. They began on the preceding Saturday with a fair (*Ffair y Bol*, lit. 'belly fair') at which nothing but eatables was sold. As part of the preparations it was customary for the well-to-do farmers to kill sheep and keep an open house, making presents to the poorer parishioners so that they too had the means of entertaining their friends who visited them. In the Gower peninsula, the *mabsant*, as it was known in Glamorgan, was renowned for the consumption of a kind of plum pudding called 'bonny clobby', made specially for the festival. The wakes at Llansanffraid-ym-Mechain, Montgomeryshire, which began on a Sunday and lasted until Wednesday or Thursday, catered for both rich and poor with an 'interlude', harp and fiddle playing, morris-dancing, a hunt and a grand ball. The poor were not forgotten, for they were provided with 'wakes' meat' on the occasion. The festival was brought to a close by the election of a 'Mayor of the Wakes':

A necessary qualification for this office was that the candidate must have spent the whole of the time from Sunday morning until Wednesday night in the public houses in a state of drunkenness without once visiting his family! When a person was found who had attained this standard, haste was made to deck him with ribbons, garlands and evergreens; he was placed in a chair, sometimes a wheelbarrow, holding a large jug in his right hand, carried up and down the village and proclaimed the Mayor of the Wakes until the next wakes.

The election of a mock mayor, in this fashion, was a common feature of rustic celebrations, symbolizing a ritual over-turning of the established order for the duration of the festivities. The practice has been recorded in Llandybïe, Carmarthenshire, in association with the fair which, as so often happened, replaced the old *gwylmabsant* of the parish, and also in Llangeitho, Cardiganshire, where the precise occasion is not noted.

Folk customs and the Church calendar

The influence of the Church, of course, extended beyond the *llan*, its services, ceremonies of birth, marriage and death, and the yearly patronal festival, to reach the entire community. Nowhere was this influence to be seen more clearly than in the traditional customs of the countryside which were linked with the ecclesiastical calendar and its major festivals. The Christmas season, *y gwyliau*, lasted not only for the traditional twelve days culminating in *Gŵyl Ystwyll* (Epiphany), but often frequently much longer. Its peripatetic customs, such as the *Mari Lwyd*, the Wren's House, the New Year's Gift (*Calennig*), New Year's Water, rivalled the religious ceremonies of the Church (apart from the *plygain*) in the popular affection. The change in the calendar in 1752, when the 'New Style' was introduced and eleven days omitted, led to considerable confusion in the dates of many popular customs. Several continued to be celebrated according to the 'Old Style' long after the change had been introduced; and the more unofficial the custom the more likely the discrepancy was to survive. Easter and its dependent sequence of popular festivals beginning with Shrove Tuesday, and culminating in Whitsuntide, were, of course, unaffected by the introduction of the new Gregorian calendar, their dates being decided by that of the first full moon on or after 21 March. The order of the Sundays in Lent leading up to Easter was memorized in the following doggerel which can be traced back to *A Dictionary in Englyshe and Welshe* published by William Salesbury in 1547:

Dydd Sul Ynyd, Dydd Sul hefyd,
Dydd Sul a ddaw, Dydd Sul gerllaw;
Dydd Sul y Meibion, Dydd Sul y Gwrychon;
Dydd Sul y Blodau, Pasg a'i ddyddiau.

(Shrove Sunday, another Sunday, Sunday which comes, Sunday at hand, the Sons' Sunday (Mothering Sunday), Peas' Sunday (Carling Sunday), Flowering Sunday, Easter and its days).

Each of the movable feasts named had its traditional customs, Eastertide being more important in Wales than the Carnival celebrations, preceding Lent, which flourished in warmer climes. According to Elias Owen, it was the practice in the Vale of Clwyd for all adults in the parish to partake of Communion but not at the same time; servants, farmers and gentry partook on different days. The afternoon of Easter Saturday was formerly a half holiday

Christmas and the 'plygain' in Dolgellau c. 1850

Now is the appointed morning. Just after five the church bells (eight) ring out, the sound of many feet, and laughs and shouts are heard in the streets. Now come into town from miles and miles around (for our parish is thirteen or fourteen miles long), old and young, Churchmen and Dissenters (Oh, the blessed day of peace, for even theology throws off its rancours for the Plygain). Now the church is in a blaze, now crammed, body, aisles, gallery, now Shon Robert, the club-footed shoemaker, and his wife, descending from the singing seat to the lower and front part of the gallery, strike up alternately, and without artificial aid of pitch pipe, the long, long carol and old favourite describing the Worship of Kings and of the Wise Men, and the Flight into Egypt, and the terrible wickedness of Herod. The crowds are wholly silent and rapt in admiration. Then the good Rector, and his curate, David Pugh, stand up, and read the Morning Service abbreviated, finishing with the prayer for All Conditions of Men, and the benediction—restless and somewhat surging is the congregation during prayers—the Rector obliged sometimes to stop short in his office and look direct at some part or persons, but no verbal admonishment. Prayers over, the singers begin again more carols, new singers, old carols in solos, duets, trios, choruses, then silence in the audience, broken at appropriate pauses by the suppressed hum, of delight and approval, till between eight and nine, hunger telling on the singers, the Plygain is over and the Bells strike out a round peal. The oatcakes in the Browas, the swig, the strong ale, the cakes, the cold meats, are soon being ravenously devoured at Dr Williams's and all his neighbours' houses, far and wide, the young ones afterwards going to football and ball playing, the other ones criticising the carols till church time and dinner come round, when feasting finishes the day.

Bye-gones, 11 September 1895.

in the district; servants claimed it as a matter of right and spent it in games, but they attended church in the morning of the day.

Easter Monday was the great gala day alike with both masters and servants. It was spent in jollity, games and exhibitions of strength and wrestling. Derwen had its *erw ysgwt* (wrestling quillet). Here also *bragod* (bragget), a mixture of mead and spiced beer, was especially prepared for Easter Monday. It was an old custom for the young women of the parish on Easter Monday to invite to the public house all the young men they met on their way to the village to have a drink of *bragod.*

Everywhere in Wales Easter marked the resumption of the pleasures of life which had been in abeyance during Lent, and the attendant customs varied from district to district, with a common revival of interest in open-air sports of all kinds and in merry-making.

5 Changing Traditions

Industrialization

The nineteenth century, when Wales felt the full blast of industrialization, should not be regarded as a period of decline in the history of our popular culture, despite the disappearance of many traditional customs. Preoccupation with the learning of the new craft skills required by the nascent industries, and the different rhythm of regular long working days, interrupted by spells of unemployment during the cyclical slumps, discouraged the continuation of many traditional practices which had made sense in the countryside. The conventions of neighbourliness changed from the sanctioned begging, scarcely concealed as folk custom, of the rural areas, to the assertive solidarity of the new unregulated settlements confronted by the truculence of the iron and coal masters. Immigrants to the boisterous 'frontier society' which had emerged on the northern rim of the coalfield in Glamorgan and Monmouthshire, found in the foot-race, the boxing booth and the beer shop more congenial ways of spending their leisure than the frequently innocuous seasonal pursuits of the countryside they had left. The new working class-in-the-making clung to such manifestations of the old popular culture as the *ceffyl pren* (or skimmington), rough music and the disguise of the 'Scotch Cattle' in its attempts to exercise social control, but became more interested, as the years passed, in the politicization of its struggle for decent working and living conditions, and, ultimately, the attainment of respectability. The means of transport were improved spectacularly in the middle of the century when the railways criss-crossed the country bringing previously remote communities within reach of the new commercial influences and undermining any tendencies towards a self-supporting economy which might previously have existed. The creation of a new educational system in the 1870s, moreover, introduced a new tendency towards uniformity in social attitudes and spread the use of the English language in hitherto monoglot Welsh districts. By the end of the nineteenth century the cumulative effects of the social forces unleashed by industrialism had pervaded the whole society.

The Methodist Revival

The transformation of Wales into an industrial society took place during a period of religious upheaval which had equally far-reaching consequences for the popular culture. The Methodist Revival first broke out in the countryside of south Wales in the 1730s and slowly penetrated the whole country by the end of the century, galvanizing an earlier tradition of religious dissent and eventually transforming the whole of Welsh cultural life. By the middle of the following century the Nonconformists had grown from a tiny minority to become a dominant force in a greatly expanded population, and had with increasing confidence set about creating their own distinctive and respectable alternative culture epitomized by the choir, the eisteddfod and the literary meeting. The influence of the Revival itself is not in dispute; what is uncertain is how far some of these changes would have occurred independently of the religious awakening of the eighteenth century, as a result of a more general process of modernization involving, at a later stage, the cumulative effects of industrialization. For the rise of an alternative popular culture in opposition to the traditional folk culture, whilst inspired by religion, was undoubtedly also influenced by industrialism. The new or revived forms were as characteristic of the industrial areas as of the countryside; indeed the sheer concentration of population facilitated the development of a flourishing choral tradition in industrial settlements such as Merthyr Tydfil, Rhosllannerchrugog and Bethesda. Furthermore, how rapidly these substantial cultural changes took place in various parts of the country, and regional differences in the response to religious changes are subjects which require further detailed investigation. It has been suggested, for example, that in south Wales secular events were more likely to be held on the old religious feast days than in north Wales by the end of the nineteenth century.

The patronal festivals of the parish churches, as we saw in the last chapter, were losing some of their cruder elements even before Methodism was powerful enough to exert any influence on them. Indeed, effective religious opposition to their excesses came from people who had scant sympathy for Methodism and what it stood for. The cleric responsible for purging the Holyhead Wakes of their 'Sundays of the Relics' in 1758, for example, was not an itinerant Methodist preacher but the Revd Thomas Ellis, a clergyman and author of an anti-Methodist tract. The opposition of such people, however, was selective, and was directed against offensive behaviour rather than supposed popish survivals. Parson Ellis, for instance, saw nothing wrong in 'kneeling on the sea shore' to ensure the success of the 'herring harvest' in a religious ceremony which would certainly not have met with the approval of Methodists. But he was also alleged in 1762 to have uprooted from the district all the old women who were able to cast spells, an achievement which later reformers might have envied. Although the influence of the Methodists on the everyday life of the island may be traced back to 1743, when the new 'enthusiasm' was introduced, it was not until the very end of the century, in the opinion of John Hughes, that 'the old pagan and popish customs of the previous age were on the verge of completely disappearing, so that there was no longer to be heard mention of evenings spent dancing or playing cards'. By then 'cock-fighting, interludes and playing hand or foot ball on the Lord's Day had been shamed out of sight, with almost nobody approving them'.

Elsewhere in Wales, it has been suggested, the old Nonconformists who had preceded Methodism (but were later influenced by it) had come to terms with the old way of life despite their inherent puritanism. W. J. Gruffydd contrasts Caernarfonshire and Anglesey, 'where puritanism came in a barer age' with Llanuwchllyn, Merioneth, with its 'delightful compromise between the old things

The slow penetration of Methodism
Although preaching by the Methodist revivalists had begun in some corner of the South and the North a hundred years ago, and more than that in some places, it did not influence the ordinary customs of the nation very much for a period of forty years after the earliest beginnings. Dawn had broken, it is true; but the mist which covered the the country had not yet dispersed. Dark clouds of deep ignorance rested on the bulk of the ordinary people until the establishment of the Sunday School. The old customs—the feats, the recital of false tales, the cock-fighting and all the associated objects, retained their strength until within the last sixty years. The numbers professing religion were still only small; the chapels were infrequent, small in size and greyish in appearance, and those professing were only recognized as the objects of persecution and contempt.

John Hughes, *Methodistiaeth Cymru*, 1854, 1, 52. (Translated)

which were loved for their pleasure and the new things which were admired for their worth'. R. T. Jenkins discerns a similar accommodation to the old order among the old Nonconformists of Glamorgan and lower Brecon. However, it is dangerous to generalize on denominational grounds, for with the passage of time Congregationalists and Baptists came to share the same strong views as Methodists on the evils of the 'depraved customs' of the past. There was no sterner critic of 'the religion of the dark ages', to use the title of his book on the *Mari Lwyd* and similar pagan or popish follies, than the Baptist William Roberts, 'Nefydd', in the middle of the nineteenth century. Nor was opposition to the unacceptable customs of the countryside by this time limited to Nonconformists, old and new. It was the vicar of Llandysul, Cardiganshire, who, in 1833, stamped out the riotous interparochial football match (*Y Bêl Ddu*) played on Old New Year's Day, and established in its place a Church Sunday School Festival.

The hearth traditions—from 'noson lawen' to prayer meeting

The influence of Methodism, which from an early stage in its development was organized on the basis on local cells (or 'societies of experience'), was exerted through itinerant preaching, generally carried on outside the usual channels of the Established Church, and to the point of saturation. The older Nonconformist churches, too, although historically more intellectual in their approach to religion, were infected by the new 'enthusiasm' and often co-operated actively with the reformers especially during the early years. The Methodist 'exhorters', who were the active agents of change in the local communities, were mostly uneducated men, and the 'societies' in their care met at first in the various homes, barns or cow-sheds belonging to the converted, before eventually building their own chapels to house the larger congregations attracted to their meetings. In the early years, the hearth tradition of the countryside, with its evening assemblies of neighbours during the winter months to engage in such sociable tasks as knitting stockings or peeling rushes, provided the revivalists with a ready audience, and it was not long before some of these peripatetic gatherings were turned into neighbourhood prayer meetings.

The *noson lawen* and the prayer meeting co-existed in many districts, with people being persuaded to forsake the former for the latter, as happened in Dolwyddelan, Caernarfonshire, in the 1780s. Indeed, a concerted attempt was made in Dolwyddelan to

101

Praying at a 'noson weu' in Llanuwchllyn in 1737
Many of the people of the neighbourhood came to the meeting, but all of them with their stockings in their hands, as
on other evenings when they went to each other's houses
(meetings to knit together are a nightly custom in this
country); they sat down thus about the floor of the house,
everybody's fingers busy at their work. In the meantime
Mr Rees was sitting near the fire, glancing through the corner of his eye at his audience. When he saw his chance
he rose from his place by the fire to the table on the side
of the floor and took the Bible in order to read a chapter,
fully expecting them to put their stockings aside to listen
to the Word of God. But they stuck to their knitting. He
took the opportunity to comment on some of the topics
of the chapter, but nothing succeeded in quietening their
fingers any more than their minds. After this ... he started
to pray, and as he went down on his knees, he saw them
knitting busily before he closed his eyes ... [but] before
he had finished [his prayer] he could hear quiet sighs from
among them; and by the time he rose from being on his
knees he could see that every stocking had fallen to the
floor.

Y Drysorfa, 1813. (Translated)

hold a prayer meeting in every house in the parish, beginning
at either end of the valley and finishing in the newly established
chapel in the middle. Even after the numerous chapels had been
built throughout Wales in the first half of the nineteenth century,
the decentralized Nonconformist tradition of holding religious
meetings in the scattered farmsteads persisted, ensuring the penetration of the new ideas and attitudes to all sections of the community. In Merioneth, for example, one Methodist minister, Ffowc
Ifans (1783–1866), had delivered over a thousand sermons in his
native parish of Llanuwchllyn, during twenty years of adulthood
before entering the full-time ministry; and his exact contemporary,
Cadwaladr Jones, later a Congregationalist minister, had preached
in every house in the same place between 1806 and 1811. John
Williams, a lay preacher in Dolwyddelan later in the century, was

said to have delivered over 6,000 sermons during his lifetime. Few people can have escaped the influence of such preachers upon their ideas and personal behaviour. In the process the sermon became virtually a conscious art-form and its more accomplished exponents became figures of national renown who were frequently lionized. However, not all the preaching was of a high standard and there are numerous references in the nineteenth century to the 'jacks' who were 'bawling uncharitable dogs' and 'unruly blockheads' in the opinion of one eminent Methodist minister, the Revd Richard Lumley. Nevertheless such constant and diligent activity, which was characteristic of the religious life of the age, could not but succeed in eliminating many frivolous and worldly elements from the traditional recreation of the hearth, while at the same time facilitating the eventual incorporation of the more acceptable elements in the new cultural tradition of the numerous chapels which were built to accommodate the flood of new members.

Chapel building

The Nonconformist chapels of the eighteenth century were mostly unpretentious buildings, sometimes converted from other uses as domestic dwellings or farm buildings. The Methodist chapel built in Dolwyddelan in 1783 was nine yards by seven in size, had an earthen floor on which rushes were strewn in winter (as in the parish churches of the period), and a chimney in one gable (allegedly so that it could be converted into a dwelling if the cause failed). It had no pews, apart from a few benches, and the pulpit consisted of part of an old tree stump. The construction was carried out by the members themselves, the timber being carried by them over a distance of two miles, and paid for by such methods as collecting bracken-ashes and selling them for export by ship from Trefriw to be used in soap-making. The chapel itself was enlarged in 1806 and subsequently replaced by a later building in 1835, at a time when Wales was experiencing a spate of chapel construction. The establishment of the Calvinistic Methodists as a separate body in 1811, and the infusion of the older Nonconformist churches with the evangelizing zeal of the revival, made the first half of the nineteenth century a period of tremendous expansion. It has been calculated that a new Congregationalist cause was established on average every five weeks between 1800 and 1850. The population of Wales doubled over the same period, and it estimated that from being a small minority at the beginning of the century, Nonconformists by 1850 accounted for eight out of ten of the inhabitants of the country. The new chapels that were built on an unprecedented scale to house this huge influx had rather more architectural pretensions but nevertheless retained some of the informality of the earlier meeting houses despite their fixed pews and 'big seat'.

Nonconformity triumphant

We now walk in the light. Fairies and ghosts have vanished. The mighty fabric of superstition, reared by the industry of ages, lies scattered in dismal and ignominious ruins. The age of the interlude and drama is gone by. The old popular amusements have become obsolete. Our corrupt national music has given way to the songs of Zion ... Point to us a nook or corner, a glen or valley, a dingle or pass, a marsh or rock, where human beings have fixed their local habitations, where they have not been followed by the gospel ... From the highest peak in the land to the lowest valleys, they have studded the country with chapels and schoolrooms ... On the altars of our sanctuaries, rustic and unadorned as they are, can be found the living fire. No brazen gates, no gorgeous avenues lead to our temples, yet angels love to linger around them. There is no spot within the Principality where the Welsh is spoken, where the people perish for the lack of knowledge.

Evan Jones, 'Ieuan Gwynedd', *The Progress of Dissent and Moral Improvement*, 1849.

Adapting funeral and carol customs

In the age-old manner of Christianity many customs practised by the community were modified so as to make them more acceptable to the chapels and their members. The *gwylnos* or funeral wake of the eighteenth century, for instance, had incorporated a number of frivolous characteristics which were felt to be out of keeping with such a solemn occasion. Besides *padreua i'r wylnos* (the reciting of the paternoster at the wake) and the singing of psalms, which were common to most parts of the country, the incongruous practice of drawing the corpse slowly up through the chimney and then gradually lowering it and replacing it in the coffin was to be found in Pembrokeshire, where it was referred to as *hir-wen-gwd* (long white bag or shroud). The origin and meaning of this peculiar custom are obscure, but, together with the common practice of lighting candles for placing at the head and foot of the body, respectively, with its 'popish' associations, it was frowned upon by Nonconformists. In many districts the *gwylnos* consequently became to all intents and purposes a prayer meeting (sometimes including a sermon) held on the evening before the funeral. Similarly, Nonconformity influenced the *offrwm* or offering, which, as we saw in the previous chapter, was made in the church during the funeral service. In the quarrying districts of Caernarfonshire, this took the form of *danfon offrwm*, i.e. taking one's offering to the house where the coffin lay, and placing a small sum on a handkerchief laid out on a round table, while a deacon or elder of the chapel stood by. Nonconformists also adopted an ambivalent attitude to the special carol services held in the parish church at Christmas time. The *plygain* in most places in north Wales was attended by chapel people, and in some districts, most Methodists retained a loose association with the parish church and attended the services at Easter, Whitsun and Christmas. Elsewhere, however, as in the Baptist church in Rhuddlan, Flintshire, the Nonconformists held a prayer meeting for their members to keep them away from the *plygain* in the parish church. In Glamorgan the *plygain* itself had been adopted by some Nonconformist chapels, together with its Christmas trimmings.

Preaching replaces feasting

More direct opposition was shown to certain customs and practices which were obnoxious to the revivalists. In Dolwyddelan, the building of the new chapel in 1783 was followed by an assault on the practice of *boddi'r cynhaeaf* (drowning the harvest) and its attendant drunkenness, which was replaced by a religious thanksgiving service in the home of a local farmer; children's Sunday games were stopped, and cock-fighting (which took place on the Sabbath) was prevented by digging up the cock-pit. Similar action was taken in many parts of the country. One of the preachers who was influential in establishing the chapel in Dolwyddelan was the Revd David Jones, Llan-gan, Glamorgan, and it was he, nearer home, who preached to the crowds attending the largest

An open-air prayer meeting held near Llyn Eiddwen, Cardiganshire, 1911.

and most famous patronal festival in the county at Peterston-super-montem in 1768, and was able to establish an annual preaching festival which subsequently supplanted the old *mabsant*. In north Wales, the Revd John Elias succeeded in a sermon delivered in 1801 in terrifying the inhabitants of Llanrhyddlad, Anglesey, who had intended performing an 'interlude' as part of the Easter celebrations. The following year, at Rhuddlan, Flintshire, he attended one of the popular hiring fairs held in that town on Sundays during the harvest period to decide *cyflog y groes* ('cross wages') and through his forceful sermon attacking the breaking of the Sabbath, put an end to the practice.

The temperance movement
Drinking was involved in many of the traditional folk customs, often as part of the hospitality offered to those participating; and drunkenness was at first deplored by the early reformers as part of a general life-style which also included other forms of reprehensible behaviour. Before his conversion in 1763 at the age of twenty-eight, for example, Owen Thomas Rowland of Anglesey was described as a foul-mouthed and wicked man who neither feared God nor respected his fellow men. He was said to spend between 30*s*. and £2—a large sum in those days—every time he went to the Sessions in Beaumaris. He could swallow two quarts of beer at a time, and generally spent the day drinking beer and the night playing cards. Such personal conduct was quite at variance with

Civilizing the neighbourhood in Pembrokeshire

One of the neighbouring clergy called Miss Thomas 'the chief civilizer of the neighbourhood' which description appeared to me, so far as I could see, to be perfectly just, her tact in dealing with the people being equal to her earnestness. On the day that I first called upon her the wedding-feast of one of her servants, who had been a teacher in the Sunday School, was being celebrated in her house. I have already spoken of the disgraceful proceedings which characterize such occasions, in my account of the adjoining parish of Begelly. The common word among the working people for such a festival is 'a spree'. This was to be an example of 'a sober spree' retaining all its characteristic customs that were harmless. I found her house full of people, all very smartly dressed, and the men mostly smoking. In the evening the bride and bridegroom held the usual feast in their own house for 'the bidding'. It is the custom for the bridesmaids to go round with plates, and empty the collections into the white apron of the bride, who stands to receive them. On this occasion £8 was so collected, a greater sum (the collier-teacher in the Sunday School told me) than could have been realized had the newly-married couple sold beer in the usual manner. Miss Thomas attended this gathering herself. In the course of it, some of the young fellows were once or twice disposed to sing the looser songs sung on such occasions. However, the girls who had been educated in the day and Sunday School, with great tact, checked the attempt by beginning to sing some of their school-tunes, especially 'Happy Land', which is a general favourite with all classes: as they could sing much better than the *mauvais sujets*, and the latter felt themselves to be in the wrong, after a little jeering at first, the whole company acquiesced and the evening passed as pleasantly as if the common licence had been permitted. I was assured that the example thus set of purifying rather than abolishing an old custom had made a deep impression in the neighbourhood.

Report on Education in Wales, 1847, Appendix, 437.

the new standards which Methodism was eager to promote among its converts. However, it was only later, in the 1830s, when tea-drinking had become a practical alternative to beer (in the absence of a sanitary water supply), that excessive drinking came to be singled out as a moral vice to be eradicated, and moderation in the consumption of alcohol, if not total abstinence, a virtue to be encouraged. The proliferation of beer houses, which was a consequence of the Beer Act of 1830, increased the facilities for the consumption of beer and greatly exacerbated the drink problem. The temperance movement, which began in earnest in 1835 with the establishment of local societies, vacillated between teetotalism and moderation as the most effective solution. The movement, which appears at first to have made greater headway in north Wales than in the south, probably because of the greater commitment of Methodist leaders such as the Revd John Elias of Anglesey, later spread to the whole of the country, eventually changing popular attitudes to what had previously been regarded as a normal and healthy part of the daily fare. Temperance festivals and processions were arranged to coincide with popular attractions where drinking was the order of the day. During the horse races at Holywell, Flintshire, in 1836, for example, thousands of people were attracted by the processions, singing and oratory organized in the town by the temperance reformers, with the result that the races were a total failure and were subsequently discontinued. In Anglesey, the first temperance wedding was held in 1838 at Llanfair Pwllgwyngyll, the 170 guests contributing the money they would in the past have spent on intoxicants towards helping the young couple. In neighbouring Bryngwran in the same year the number of public houses was reduced from thirteen to four. Elsewhere the *cwrw bach* or bid ale held for the benefit of the poor or sick gave place to the tea party. This happened in Carmarthen in 1859, for example, where admission was by means of a ticket costing a shilling, with 'tea on the table at four o'clock'; the tea party on this occasion was for the benefit of a newly-married couple who had moved in to their new home.

Nonconformist counter-culture

The most fascinating aspect of the growing dominance of the chapel in the course of the century was the way in which a new counter-culture evolved which catered for the thousands who were drawn into the orbit of Nonconformist religion. From the outset the chapels had had a somewhat relaxed and homely atmosphere.

The visiting preacher at Esgairdawe chapel in Carmarthenshire, for example, partook of his dinner of bread, cheese and beer, before the fire in the chapel itself, and was joined in the meal by the family responsible for hospitality during the month in question. He would then enjoy a pipeful of tobacco in the chapel before leaving for his afternoon engagement elsewhere. Societies and activities of all kinds were established as part of chapel life. Some were charitable in purpose, such as the clothing club set up in Henllan Amgoed, Carmarthenshire, in 1844. Others were broader in scope; the popular lecture, for instance, became a feature of the chapel in the same period, together with cultural and literary societies, socials and 'penny readings' some of which had an educational as well as a broadly religious and social purpose.

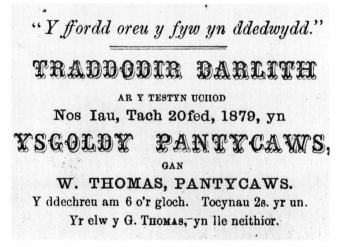

"Y ffordd oreu y fyw yn ddedwydd."

TRADDODIR DARLITH

AR Y TESTYN UCHOD

Nos Iau, Tach 20fed, 1879, yn

YSGOLDY PANTYCAWS,

GAN

W. THOMAS, PANTYCAWS.

Y ddechreu am 6 o'r gloch. Tocynau 2s. yr un.

Yr elw y G. Thomas, yn lle neithior.

Admission ticket to a lecture on 'The Best Way to Live Happily' held in a chapel school-room in 1879 as a substitute for a bidding to assist a newly-married man.

The most fundamental of these institutions, however, was the Sunday school which had begun in the 1780s with the aim of teaching not only Bible-reading but also the rudiments of civil behaviour. Although opposed by many at first as breaking the Sabbath, the movement rapidly gained ground as its potential for religious education, and in particular the study (and the learning by heart)

Nazareth Chapel Sunday School Class, Talybont, Cardiganshire, c. *1897.*

of the Scriptures was realized. By the end of the century there were nearly seven times as many Sunday-school teachers as there were day-school teachers in Wales, and in the three historical counties of Gwynedd fifty-eight per cent of the entire population attended Sunday school, the largest single school being that of Salem Chapel, Caernarfon with 940 members. Ideally, each Sunday school had six grades, including adult classes. In fact, over sixty per cent of those attending in Anglesey and Merioneth at the beginning of the present century were over the age of fifteen. As a powerful force making for literacy, the Sunday school underpinned the broad range of activities which the Victorian chapels organized for their members in the new schoolrooms and vestries built to house them, and which spilled over into the life of the community.

Hymn-singing and the choral tradition
The importance of choral music in this new counter-culture is perhaps its best-known feature outside Wales. The hymn-singing tradition out of which this developed had its origin in the fervour of the Methodist Revival and the impromptu rejoicing which fol-

lowed an inspiring sermon. It was not unusual in these circumstances for a single verse to be sung over and over again as many as thirty or forty times. The use of musical instruments was prohibited, and hymn-singing, although commonly found, was not respected as an integral part of the service, people often entering the chapel during the singing of the first hymn and leaving during the last. The emergence of a disciplined singing tradition as part of a more formal religious service was a slow process requiring both suitable hymns and tunes. The words of William Williams, 'Pantycelyn', provided the former, and folk songs, English tunes and psalm melodies the latter. Interestingly enough, despite the existence of divergent strongly-held theological views, the movement to improve congregational singing was for many years non-denominational. The Society of Religious Singers, established in Bethesda, Caernarfonshire, in 1828, was the first of several such societies. Its members, who met on a Saturday evening to rehearse the hymns to be sung at Carneddi Methodist Chapel the following day, were drawn from all denominations and included some who later became composers of hymn tunes, such as William Owen, Prysgol, who wrote the well-known 'Bryn Calfaria'. In the chapels themselves the hymns were sung two lines at a time, a practice which sometimes survived the introduction of hymn-books which had made it superfluous. The powerful religious revival of 1859, which attracted yet more to the chapels, coincided with the introduction of the tonic sol-fa notation which greatly facilitated the reading of music by untrained congregations. The 'modulator' sheet henceforth became a permanent fixture on the walls of chapel schoolrooms, and both adults and children were instructed in its use in the 'singing school' usually held after the Sunday evening service. The *cymanfa ganu*, or singing festival, of which the first was held in Aberystwyth in 1830, was given a new impetus in the 1860s by John Roberts, 'Ieuan Gwyllt', who made extensive use of the new notation. The popularity of the singing festival spread to all parts of Wales, especially at Easter and Whitsun, the usual practice being to hold three sessions, the morning session being intended for the children. In 1895 it was estimated that 280 singing festivals were held in the course of that year by the Nonconformist churches and that 134,550 persons took part—nearly nine per cent of the total population. This does not include the singing and choral festivals of the Established Church, which had also benefited from the musical revival. By the end of the century it was not uncommon for chapel choirs to present oratorios at Christmas and Easter, especially in the more populous industrial communities.

Dr R. Tudur Jones has analysed the evidence relating to 114 chapels in Swansea which submitted evidence in 1905 to the Royal Commission on the Church of England and other Religious Bodies in Wales and Monmouthshire. As many as sixty-seven of the chapels had a choir, and five of these had two choirs. Two chapels performed three works annually, and a large number presented one every year, the weekly practices, of course, adding to the already numerous activities held in the chapel. Dr Jones cites the example of Libanus Welsh Baptist Chapel where the following evening meetings were held: Monday, prayer meeting and temperance meeting; Tuesday, band of hope and Christian Endeavour; Wednesday, 'society'; Thursday, women's prayer meeting, and the choir; Friday, Bible class; Saturday, men's prayer meeting. The chapels belonging to the other Nonconformist denominations, Dr Jones points out, followed the same pattern.

The growth of the eisteddfod

The musical tradition which had been nurtured in the chapels also found expression in the eisteddfod, particularly in the choral competitions and concerts which became the major attractions of the festival in the second half of the century. Although the Llangollen Eisteddfod of 1858, which lasted four days, and to which crowds, for the first time, were brought by excursion trains, was in many respects the first modern eisteddfod, it was in the 1860s that the current practice of holding the national festival alternately in north and south Wales began. Choirs of several hundred voices, drawing on the resources of the new industrial areas, were able to compete not only in Wales but in festivals further afield such as that held in the Crystal Palace in 1872 where a choir of 456 under the baton of Griffith Rhys Jones, 'Caradog', succeeded in winning the trophy. That the eisteddfod at both national and local levels was more successful in promoting choral and vocal music than it was in creating a new orchestral tradition was probably because of its dependence on the training in singing which its competitors had received in the chapels and their festivals in which musical instruments played no part. Even the organ and harmonium were not to be found in the chapels until the second half of the last century, and the harp, like much of the traditional music and dance of Wales, had been banished to the tavern to return eventually to the eisteddfod and concert platform.

Trophy won at a competition held at the Crystal Palace, London, in 1872,
by a choir of 456 members from various parts of south Wales conducted
by Griffith Rhys Jones, 'Caradog', (1834–97), of Aberdare, Glamorgan.

The survival of ancient customs

While the chapels came to accept and promote music and literature on their own terms, there were other features of the traditional culture which survived and developed beyond reach of their influence and often in spite of their opposition. To ignore these would be to present an unbalanced picture of the popular culture of modern Wales, for these, too, filled the void left by the disappearance of so many traditional customs. Sometimes they took over earlier practices and gave them a new purpose. An interesting example of this was noted in 1853 in Defynnog, Breconshire, where an old May Day custom had been transformed into a Friendly Society procession in the 1840s. Two boys, representing the King of Winter and the King of Summer, elaborately dressed in birchen boughs and wearing crowns of holly and coloured ribbons, respectively, were each carried in a semi-recumbent position by four men. The procession, led by two men with drawn swords and including 'the general assemblage of men and boys', called at all the respectable houses in and around the village, receiving gifts of money or beer, and finally entered the churchyard, where they dispersed after the two Kings had received sums of money. The custom, which is reminiscent of the medieval tradition of a struggle between Winter and Summer on May Day, had 'merged into an Ivorite club (commenced four years previously) which still walks on the same day, and prospers to the great benefit of the members'. The Friendly Societies, like the Temperance Societies which flourished in the same period, engaged in processions in which banners and sometimes regalia were carried. Like the numerous societies associated with the chapels, they were an expression of the spirit of the new age.

Old traditions and new laws

The formalization of age-old ceremonies and the extension of secular civil authority to what had previously been religious occasions marked another change in Victorian society which influenced many traditional customs. Hardwick's Marriage Act of 1753 had indeed strengthened the sacred nature of matrimony by restricting the contracting of marriage to the parish church. It also promoted the practice of holding 'biddings' in aid of newly-wed couples by making illegal those clandestine and temporary marriages which had undermined the certainty of repayment essential to those occasions. After 1753 the *priodas fawr* (big wedding) solemnized in the parish church replaced its rival the *priodas fach* (little wedding) celebrated without benefit of clergy, often in a *noson lawen*. With the passing of legislation enabling the solemnization of marriages in chapels and registry offices after 1837, the term *priodas fach* acquired a new meaning and came to refer to the civil ceremony.

The setting up of a county constabulary, which became obligatory after 1856, led to the discontinuing of informal disciplinary practices such as the *ceffyl pren*, and boisterous customs such as the *cwrw bach* and the *Mari Lwyd*, the appearance of the latter in a state of inebriation on a country road often frightening newcomers to a district.

Modern communication and cultural change

These changes symbolized the emergence of modern Welsh society which was to indulge in other interests as it changed dramatically in size and geographical distribution and distanced itself from the unorganized and informal pastimes of the countryside. The same railway network which had enabled the eisteddfod and its competing choirs to travel with unprecedented ease to most parts of Wales made it possible to arrange football fixtures over a large geographical area as the new sport of rugby gained ground in Wales after 1875, when the South Wales Football Club was established. It has been pointed out that rugby was a middle-class game which was subsequently taken up (and indeed taken over) by the rapidly expanding working class of industrial south Wales. Its middle-class origin gave it an aura of respectability at a critical stage in its development, but like other secular activities in the same period it did not find favour with the chapels. Together with athletic sports, lawn tennis clubs, dancing clubs, singing saloons and chess tournaments—but more than any of them— football of both varieties was attacked both for its occasional violence and for the opportunities it offered for drinking. The new football clubs met in the public houses, and the chapel leaders of the closing years of the century had forgotten how indebted their forbears had been to the taverns in whose 'long rooms' many of the congregations in the industrial valleys had met before building their own meeting houses. The chapel representatives of Ystradgynlais, Breconshire, went as far as to uproot the goal posts the night before the first game of the new rugby club!

Railway excursions, whether to a football match or to the seaside, were fraught with temptation outside the restraining influence of the local community. Furthermore, new secular attractions such as the music hall, the boxing match (with its roots in the prize matches of the beginning of the century), the working men's clubs (with their alternatives to the chapels' activities), and greyhound and pigeon racing (the worker's alternatives to the turf) made rapid progress, challenging the counter-culture which the chapels had created to replace the old traditional folk culture. Other modernizing forces in social life which emerged in the twentieth

---

Boxing on the mountain in the Rhondda at the turn of the century

These fights were usually arranged in a public house on a Saturday night, more or less secretly, since the law prohibited them. It was agreed to meet in a specified place on the mountain at daybreak the following day, lest the police catch them. Although the fight was to be kept a secret, the word quietly got around, and early on Sunday morning there would be scores, if not hundreds sometimes, assembled to see the fight. On the edge of the crowd there would be a spy to keep a look-out for the men in blue. If danger appeared on the horizon, the shout 'Police!' was given, and everybody fled swiftly over the fields to the valley below, so that it was difficult to catch any of them. Those most likely to be caught were the two fighters, naked to the waist, and too tired to flee like the rest. There was not much order in keeping rounds, in all probability. But sometimes there would be a pause when the two fighters were tired out until they could hardly stand on their feet, but neither willing to yield to the other. Then, having revived a little, they would pitch in again in another bout until they were nearly exhausted, until one of them in the end had to give in. There was no referee except the shout of the rough crowd which was half demented by the excitement. It was for a golden sovereign, no more and no less, that they usually fought. As far as I heard there was not much betting among the crowds on these contests. That strange character the bookie had not reached the civilization of the South at that time.

D. J. Williams, *Yn Chwech ar Hugain Oed*, 1959, 119–120. (Translated)

century, such as the cinema, television and the increasing ease of travel, played their fateful part in the process of cultural change and were augmented by the baleful results of industrial depression, rural depopulation and war. Welsh popular culture changed almost beyond recognition in response to these influences, assimilating new ideas and expressing itself in new ways far removed from many of the customs and traditions discussed in this volume.

6 Studying Folk Customs

Early recorders of folk culture

Interest in the traditional customs of Wales predates the social and cultural changes set in train by the twin forces of the Industrial Revolution and the Methodist Revival and may be traced back to the antiquarianism of the eighteenth century and ultimately to the Renaissance itself. The discovery of the ordinary people and their culture as the objects of intellectual curiosity was a European phenomenon during this period and part of a wider fascination with the past. Edward Lhuyd (1660–1709) the polymath who laid the foundations of Celtic studies, was responsible for the earliest recording of certain folk customs (such as the hunting of the wren) through the replies received to his *Parochial Queries* of 1696. During the following century the two Anglesey brothers Lewis Morris (1701–65) and Richard Morris (1703–79) made substantial contributions to our knowledge of the folk culture of their native county. Lewis, for example, left us an important list of the Anglesey customs of the period, as well as describing, in the pages of the *Gentleman's Magazine*, some of the customs of his adopted county of Cardiganshire. His younger brother placed us in his debt through his compilation of wassail songs and similar folk poetry collected during his youth. The prolific correspondence carried on by the Morris brothers, including the botanist, William Morris (1705–63), with other antiquarians throughout Wales, reflects the great attraction exerted by the re-discovered past and by philology and ancient manuscripts, in particular, as the key to an understanding of that past.

A parallel development in England resulted in the publication of John Brand's *Observations on Popular Antiquities* in an enlarged edition in 1813 under the editorship of Sir Henry Ellis, Keeper of Manuscripts in the British Museum and Secretary of the Society of Antiquaries. This expanded work, an omnium gatherum brought out under the aegis of the scholarly establishment, incorporated not only the *Antiquitates Vulgares* of Henry Bourne, which had first appeared in 1725, but also numerous extracts from, and references to, the writings of scholars from all parts of Britain, including Lewis Morris. The field of 'popular antiquities' was henceforth recognized as an object of scholarly endeavour, Brand's sub-title, 'chiefly illustrating the origin of our Vulgar Customs, ceremonies and Superstitions' indicating its predominantly anti-quarian interest. In 1815 there appeared a volume which purported to deal with the same subject in Wales. *The Cambrian Popular Antiquities, or An Account of Some Traditions, Customs, and Super-stitions of Wales, with Observations as to their Origin, &c. &c.* was written by Peter Roberts (1760–1819), rector of Llanarmon Dyffryn Ceiriog, Denbighshire, at the request of a London book-seller who doubtless realized the popularity of the subject. Roberts's book, however, is far less comprehensive in its coverage and makes up in speculation for what it lacks in detail. Its subse-quent translation and publication by Hugh Hughes in 1823 (in a slightly different version) as *Yr Hynafion Cymreig*, brought the subject to the attention of a Welsh-reading public. The influence of Roberts's work, however, was far less than that of his near-contemporary, Edward Williams (1747–1826), better known by his bardic name Iolo Morganwg. Iolo's wayward genius revealed itself in many ways, not only as the creator of the modern *Gorsedd* of bards on the basis of his vision of the ancient literary tradition of his beloved Glamorgan, but also as the recorder of folk tra-ditions. Like Lewis Morris, he, too, left us, among his numerous manuscripts, lists of the old customs and festivals of his native county.

During this period, also, accounts of these customs appeared in the county histories alongside descriptions of material remains and other antiquities. The two volumes of *The History of the County of Brecknock* by Theophilus Jones, published in 1805 and 1809, respectively, contain much that is informative on the subject, as does Samuel Rush Meyrick's *History and Antiquities of the County of Cardigan* which appeared in 1808. Later in the century, when local history began to be written, the same service to posterity was performed in such works as *Hanes Plwyf Llandys-sul* by W.J.Davies which was published in 1896. Often the parish historians relate their accounts to those of the county historians, filling in local detail. During the second half of the nineteenth century much important material was published in the local news-papers and sometimes reprinted separately. The most important of these is undoubtedly *Bye-gones relating to Wales and the Border Counties* which first appeared in 1871 and was based on the columns of the *Oswestry Advertizer*. In the Welsh language similar material, with a more literary bias, appeared in *Y Brython* between 1858 and 1860 during the editorship of Daniel Silvan Evans (1818-1903) who later became Professor of Welsh at the University College of Wales, Aberystwyth. Folklore, as Popular Antiquities had by then become known, did not, however, become a university subject but remained, as in England, the domain of the interested amateur whose major contribution lay in the invaluable information which he collected about traditional customs apparently about to disappear for ever rather than in his attempts to explain them.

D. Silvan Evans and 'Llên y Werin'

The English have a kind of literature they call Folk lore which can be translated as *Llên y Werin*, and it has been much cultivated by them for many years. This branch of literature includes traditions, country tales, particular customs and ceremonies, superstitions and similar things, which were formerly, or which are at this time, common among the ordinary folk. There is probably not a part of the kingdom which has more of these interesting things than the Principality of Wales, and although we do not have either a well of Baranton with its Countess full of charm, and a Forest of Proseliand swarming with fairies, there is no well or river or mountain peak or verdant copse or partly concealed cave to which no superstition or tradition has belonged from time beyond memory. And when we remember that it was the tales and country and folk traditions of Wales which gave birth to the Mabinogion and initiated Fiction and Romance on the continent of Europe, we are of the opinion that we cannot do better than to set aside a corner of *Y Brython* to record from time to time as much as possible of the recesses of the Lore of the Welsh Folk in Gwynedd and Deheubarth [South Wales] before it is all completely swallowed up by the insatiable greed of loss and oblivion.

Y Brython, 1859. (Translated)

Nineteenth-century anthropology

One of the major characteristics of nineteenth-century scholarship in this field was the belief that the traditional customs which flourished (or at least survived) among the ordinary people, or folk, constituted important evidence of the earlier development of our society. It was firmly believed that they were in their own right antiquities which had been in existence from time immemorial; moreover, if their constituent elements could be unravelled and their hidden meanings exposed, scholars would be in a better position to understand the more primitive culture of our distant ancestors. It was further assumed that the more exotic and irrational behaviour associated with these popular customs was anachronistic and for that reason could be regarded, in conjunction with other more obvious survivals (such as prehistoric artefacts), as a reliable basis for conjecture about the nature of man's early history. The fact that they did not seem to belong to contemporary life made these picturesque practices even more fascinating to Victorian scholars who were not averse to seeing revealing resemblances between the folk customs of their own society on the one hand and the ceremonies of savage tribes recorded by intrepid explorers and missionaries on the other. Similarly, the compilation of data from classical antiquity provided another convenient source of comparative material. In an intellectual climate dominated by ideas on evolution and an emphasis on historical (if often speculative) interpretation, eighteenth century antiquarianism merged with the new evolutionary anthropology of the nineteenth century. E. B. Tylor, one of the founding fathers of the new discipline, was quick to see the significance of the older customs recorded by contemporary folklorists of which similar examples were to be found in different cultures throughout the world. Apparently meaningless peasant practices to Tylor were survivals which had 'fallen into absurdity from having be carried on into a new state of society where the original sense had been discarded'. Folklore collecting thus came to have a place in the broad strategy of anthropological research, and scholars like Sir James Frazer, with their use of folklore parallels across time and space, showed the significance of the material collected.

The National Eisteddfod and The Folklore Society

A peculiarly Welsh method of collecting folklore which developed in this period was the eisteddfod competition which was organized annually, usually on a county basis. One of the regular adjudicators of the competition at the National Eisteddfod was Sir John Rhŷs (1840–1914), Professor of Celtic at Oxford, who was also a Vice-President of The Folklore Society which had been established in London in 1878. Perhaps the best known of the successful collections was that of Elias Owen (1833–99), whose *Welsh Folk-*

Revd Elias Owen and the collection of folklore

By his journeys he became acquainted with many people in North Wales, and he hardly ever failed in obtaining from them much singular and valuable information of bye-gone days, which there and then he jotted down on scraps of paper afterwards transferred to note books which are still in his possession. It was his custom, after the labour of school inspection was over, to ask the clergy with whom he was staying to accompany him to the most aged inhabitants of their parish. This they willingly did, and often in the dark winter evenings, lantern in hand, they sallied forth on their journey, and in this way a rich deposit of traditions and superstitions was struck and rescued from oblivion. Not a few of the clergy were themselves in full possession of all the quaint sayings and Folk-lore of their parishes, and they were not loath to transfer them to the writer's keeping.

Elias Owen, *Welsh Folklore*, 1896 edn., iv.

lore won the prize at the London National Eisteddfod in 1887 and was published in 1896.

Sir John Rhŷs's *Celtic Folklore Welsh and Manx* appeared in two volumes in 1901 and drew upon his work during the previous thirty years in philology and archaeology as well as folklore. The link with the Folklore Society was maintained in the volume entitled *Folk-Lore and Folk-Stories of Wales* by Marie Trevelyan which appeared in 1909 with the assistance of Sidney Hartland, a prominent member of the Society. Trevelyan's book is notable for its use of information collected from among members of the author's household in addition to written sources. Jonathan Ceredig Davies, whose *Folk-Lore of West and Mid-Wales* was published in 1911, was also a member of the Folklore Society. Perhaps the most exotic writer in this field was William Wirt Sikes, US consul at Cardiff, who wrote *British Goblins: Welsh Folk-lore, Fairy Mythology, Legends, and Traditions*, published in 1880, a colourful and informative study drawing upon both oral and written material. In these various forms the second half of the nineteenth century, and the first decade of the twentieth, saw the amassing of folklore material in Wales as well as a number of attempts to study the results in a scholarly fashion. What is in many ways the most successful study in this field appeared some years later in 1930 when T.Gwynn Jones, Professor of Welsh at the University College of Wales, Aberystwyth, brought out his *Welsh Folklore and Folk Custom*, a book which remains invaluable and which was subsequently re-issued in 1979 with additional material. It was a former student of Gwynn Jones, Iorwerth C. Peate—a disciple of the pioneer geographer and anthropologist H.J.Fleure—who was responsible for inaugurating the programme of recording and research undertaken by staff of the Welsh Folk Museum in the field of folk life studies, including folk customs, after the establishment of that institution in 1948.

Human geography and ethnology

The human geography which had been established in 1918 by H. J. Fleure as an academic subject at the University College of Wales, Aberystwyth, took a broad view of human endeavour against the background of the physical environment which was regarded as a factor deeply influencing (but not determining) its historical development. Distinctive Welsh traditions had survived partly as a result of their isolation from outside influences by geographical factors. Alwyn D. Rees in his pioneering study *Life in a Welsh Countryside: A Social Study of Llanfihangel yng Ngwynfa* published in 1950 examined a Montgomeryshire community as a typical manifestation of Welsh rural culture in the broadest sense. Looking at Llanfihangel as an anthropologist might look at a primitive community, he emphasized not so much the individual customs, as a folklorist might have done, but the various ways in which these customs were intertwined as traditions which could often be traced back to early times. The economy, house and hearth, farmsteads, the family and kindred, and the other aspects of social life which he discussed, all exemplified this persistence at the local level which he regarded as a significant feature of Welsh culture. One of the reasons for this persistence was the decentralization typical of Welsh life through the ages, coupled with the absence of a strong native urban tradition.

This view was shared by E. G. Bowen who occupied Fleure's chair of Geography and Anthropology at Aberystwyth and was one of his most distinguished students. To him, however, the cause of this decentralization was directly geographical and derived from the existence of the central mountain core of Wales which had prevented each of the four petty kingdoms of the early medieval period from gaining ascendancy over its rivals and establishing a stable political unit covering the entire country. Moreover, the existence of this central core had resulted in the emergence of an Inner and an Outer Wales each with its own culture. The first comprised the north and west of the country and the second the south and east, the decisive factor being the accessibility of the latter to influences from England. The persistence of customs and traditions (including the Welsh language) in Inner Wales, according to this view, could be explained in geographical terms, with mountains acting as barriers and valleys and lowlands as access routes. Englishries and Welshries in the conquered zones of Anglo-Norman Wales reflected a similar dichotomy at the local level with the latter generally occupying the less fertile upland territory. E. G. Bowen discerned the same dualism in medieval agriculture with the manorial system and its greater emphasis on arable farming in Outer Wales contrasting with the more pastoral tradition of the native territory of Inner Wales. The dispersed habitat of the Inner zone with its isolated farmsteads likewise contrasted with the nucleated village settlements of some of the fringe areas of Outer Wales such as the Vale of Glamorgan. Even the religious situation in post-Reformation times reflected the same basic dualism, early Dissent being restricted for the most part to Outer Wales, whereas Inner Wales had to wait until the Methodist Revival for its own religious awakening. Industrialization in the nineteenth century furthermore served to reinforce the same division, for in both north and south, the new settlements sprang up largely in the Outer zone. As seen by the geographer this was the dominant physical framework within which Welsh life had existed over the centuries with its rich local variation reflected in such features as dialect differences in the Welsh language or the regional diversity of its vernacular architecture.

Wales also exists, of course, in a wider European context sharing many of its general cultural features with continental countries. A common religious heritage, profoundly modified by the Reformation and subsequent movements, formed part of the 'Great Tradition' which overlay the entire continent but manifested itself in a variety of forms at the local level. Early twentieth-century ethnologists were fascinated by the degree of variation which was to be seen in all aspects of culture, both material and non-material, and were concerned to identify areas of cultural similarity and to trace processes of diffusion in an attempt to outline the course of cultural development. Like the prehistoric archaeologist, the ethnologist came to use the distribution map extensively as part of his method of study, especially in continental Europe where linguistic and cultural boundaries frequently overlapped political divisions. Less use was made of the ethnological atlas approach in the study of customs and traditions in Britain itself, partly because of the smaller geographical scale of the country, and partly because the detailed information necessary for the compilation of such maps was not available. Two important exceptions in Wales, however, are vernacular architecture and regional dialects, both of which have been extensively documented in this fashion. Nevertheless, the emphasis in the study of folk life in Wales in all its aspects has been on the existence of marked local variations in the 'Little Tradition' to be found among the ordinary people.

Selected Reading List by Chapter

General

The general historical background is covered by the companion volume in this series by J. Graham Jones, *A Pocket Guide: The History of Wales*, 1990, and its guide to further reading. Some of the major contributions in the field covered by the present volume are mentioned in the text, especially Chapter 6. Besides these, Alwyn and Brinley Rees, *Celtic Heritage*, 1961, which discusses the mythological traditions behind many Welsh customs should be mentioned. T. M. Owen, *Welsh Folk Customs*, 1959, deals more comprehensively with some customs than is possible in the present volume. The journals *Gwerin* (1956–62), *Folklife* (1963 on), *Folklore* (1888 on) contain much relevant Welsh material as well as other ethnological and folklore articles. The magazine *Llafar Gwlad* (1983 on) includes Welsh-language contributions to this field. For a concise guide to source material housed in the Welsh Folk Museum, St Fagans, Cardiff, see A. Lloyd Hughes, 'The Welsh Folk Museum Manuscripts', *Folklife*, 17 (1979).

1 Working the Land

Elwyn Davies, 'Hafod and Lluest: The Summering of Cattle and Upland Settlement in Wales', *Folklife*, 23 (1985), also contains references to his studies of the *hafod* in various Welsh counties. F. V. Emery's volume *Wales*, 1969, in 'The World's Landscapes' is an excellent introduction to the evolution of the Welsh countryside. The exploitation of peat is further discussed in several articles by T. M.Owen: 'Peat cutting in Wales: A Socio-Technical System', in A. Gailey and A. Fenton (eds.), *The Spade in Northern and Atlantic Europe*, 1970; 'Historical Aspects of Peat-cutting in Wales' in J. G. Jenkins (ed.), *Studies in Folk Life: Essays in Honour of Iorwerth C. Peate*, 1966, and *Torri Mawn*, 1990. S. M. Tibbott's articles in *Folklife* are relevant to this chapter: 'Knitting Stockings in Wales—A Domestic Craft', 16 (1978); 'Sucan and Llymru in Wales', 12 (1974); 'Liberality and Hospitality: Food as Communication in Wales', 24 (1985–6). See also T. M. Owen, 'The Ethnological Study of Food in Wales' in C. Ó Danachair (ed.) *Folk and Farm: Essays in Honour of A. T. Lucas*, 1976. David Jenkins, *The Agricultural Community in South-West Wales at the Turn of the Twentieth Century*, 1971, contains a fascinating discussion of tenant–farmer relations; see also T. M. Owen, 'The Social Organization of Harvesting: a Welsh case-study', in H. Cheape (ed.) *Studies in European Ethnology*, 1991. For William Williams's account of a labourer's domestic economy see 'Coffadwriaethol Hanes fy Ewythr Huw Rolant a Modryb Marsli', *Anglesey Antiquarian Society Transactions*, 1932.

2 Customs of Hearth and Home

Eurwyn Wiliam, '*Yr Aelwyd*: the architectural development of the hearth in Wales', *Folklife*, 16 (1978), contains an extended treatment of the subject; I. C. Peate, *The Welsh House*, 1940, is the pioneer work in this field. See also T. M. Owen, 'Social Perspectives in Welsh Vernacular Architecture', in D. Moore (ed.), *The Irish Sea Province in Archaeology and History*, 1970; 'Cottage and Stable-loft: the relevance of non-material evidence in the study of material culture', *Archaeologia Cambrensis*, 138 (1989); 'Welsh Cottages—the Literary Evidence', in A. Gailey and D. Óh Ógáin, *Gold Under the Furze*, 1982; 'The Ritual Entry to the House in Wales', in V. Newall (ed.), *Folklore Studies in the Twentieth Century*, 1981; 'The Celebration of Candlemas in Wales', *Folklore*, 84 (1973). W. Glyn Griffiths, 'Môn', *Anglesey Antiquarian Society Transactions*, 1941, Sir Henry Jones, *Old Memories*, 1922, and S. J. Pratt, *Gleanings from Wales, Holland and Westphalia*, 1797, contain the interesting descriptions of domestic interiors referred to in this chapter.

3 Community Traditions

The poverty of the age is discussed in W. J. Lewis, 'Labour in Mid-Cardiganshire in the early nineteenth century', *Ceredigion*, 4 (1960–3), and is the background of Hugh Evans, *Cwm Eithin*, 1931, translated as *The Gorse Glen*. The account of the *cyvarfod cymorth* is taken from *The Cambro-briton* (1822) and that of the *pastai* in the Swansea Valley from a BBC TV interview in 1963 by Mrs Elizabeth Edwards. For a fuller treatment of wedding customs see T. M. Owen, 'A Breconshire Marriage Custom', *Folklore*, 72 (1961), and 'Some Aspects of the Bidding in Cardiganshire', *Ceredigion*, 4 (1960). A brief discussion of the *tŷ unnos* occurs in T. M. Owen, 'Social Perspectives in Welsh Vernacular Architecture' (see Chapter 2). D. J. V. Jones's *Before Rebecca*, 1973, and *Rebecca's Children*, 1990, contain excellent analyses of the Scotch Cattle and the rural unrest of the mid-nineteenth century, and on the latter subject David Williams, *The Rebecca Riots*, 1955, is also essential reading. W. T. R. Pryce and T. A. Davies, *Samuel Roberts Clockmaker: an Eighteenth Century Craftsman in a Welsh Rural Community*, 1985, contains one of the few references to clock clubs. The criticism of the operation of some of these clubs is taken from E. Pierce, *Nanw ach Robert*, ?1880, an historical novel based on oral tradition in the Dolwyddelan district of Caernarfonshire, to which other references are made elsewhere in this book. The Anglesey diaries of Robert Bulkeley and William Bulkeley referred to here and in the next chapter are reproduced in the *Anglesey Antiquarian Society Transactions* for 1937 and 1931 respectively. Traditional games are discussed in H. Lloyd, 'Tri o Chwareuon Cymru' and H. M. Waddington, 'Games and Athletics in Bygone Wales' in the *Transactions of the Honourable Society of Cymmrodorion*, for 1960 and 1953 respectively, and T. V. Jones, 'Handball and Fives', *Medel*, 1 (1985), 22–7. G. J. Williams, 'Glamorgan Customs in the Eighteenth Century', *Gwerin*, 1 (1956–7), deals with the *taplas haf* and gambols.

4 Church Festivals and Practices

E. G. Bowen's work on the Celtic saints is to be found in his *Saints, Seaways and Settlements in the Celtic Lands*, 1969, and Professor Wendy Davies's discussion in her *Wales in the Early Middle Ages*, 1982. Glanmor Williams, *The Welsh Church from Conquest to Reformation*, 1962, is the authoritative volume on the later period. Francis Jones, *The Holy Wells of Wales*, 1954, gives a comprehensive account of its subject. Most of Elias Owen's material quoted in this chapter and elsewhere in this book is taken from his *Old Stone Crosses of the Vale of Clwyd*, 1886, which is wider in scope than its title suggests. A. O. Chater's researches on 'Early Cardiganshire Gravestones' are to be found in *Archaeologia Cambrensis* 125 (1976) and 126 (1977). The discussion of the 1575 pew dispute involving the Penrhyn family is based on E .G. Jones, 'A Llandygai Pew Dispute', *Caernarvonshire Historical Society Transactions*, 9 (1948). John Fisher, 'The Welsh Calendar', in the *Transactions of the Cymmrodorion Society*, 1894–5, is still useful in understanding the main religious festivals.

5 Changing Traditions

Canon Gwynfryn Richards has contributed greatly to our understanding of many ecclesiastical traditions in his articles on 'Y Plygain' and 'Yr Offrwm Angladdol' in the *Journal of the Historical*

Society of the Church in Wales, 1 (1947) and 2 (1950), and in his chapters 'Yr Wylnos' and 'Hen Glochyddion Cymru' in *Ar Lawer Trywydd*, 1973. John Hughes, *Methodistiaeth Cymru*, 1854, is early enough to be able to rely on oral tradition for his history of Methodism some of which is used in this chapter. Anthony Jones, *Welsh Chapels*, 1984, deals with the architectural tradition. T. M. Owen, 'Chapel and Community in Glan-llyn, Merioneth', in E. Davies and A. D. Rees, *Welsh Rural Communities*, 1960, deals with the transformation of the hearth meeting. W. R. Lambert's *Drink and Sobriety in Victorian Wales c. 1820–c. 1895*, 1983, charts the rise of temperance and its antagonism to many traditional customs. Dr R. Tudur Jones's two volumes, *Ffydd ac Argyfwng Cenedl*, 1981, deal comprehensively with the relationship between Christianity and culture in Wales between 1890 and 1914. The Sunday school statistics in this chapter are taken from his *Yr Ysgol Sul: Coleg y Werin*, 1985. See also T. M. Owen, *What happened to Welsh Folk Customs?*, (The Folklore Society: The Katherine Briggs Lecture 1984). R. D. Griffith, *Hanes Canu Cynnulleidfaol Cymru*, 1948, and more recently Alan Luff, *Welsh Hymns and their Tunes*, 1990, deal with the development of the hymn-singing tradition of Wales. As a social history, D. Smith and G. Williams, *Fields of Praise*, 1980, is a highly readable account of the development of rugby football in Wales.

6 Studying Folk Customs

H. Owen, *The Life and Works of Lewis Morris 1701–65, 1951*, and T. H. Parry-Williams (ed.), *Llawysgrif Richard Morris o Gerddi &c.*, 1931, deal with two of the brothers whose prolific correspondence is contained in J. H. Davies (ed.), *The Letters of Lewis, Richard, William and John Morris of Anglesey. (Morrisiaid Môn), 1728–65*, 2 vols., 1907–9, and H. Owen (ed.), *Additional Letters of the Morrises of Anglesey (1735–1786)*, 2 vols., 1947–9. G. J. Williams, *Iolo Morganwg*, 1956, is the standard work in Welsh on Edward Williams, but Prys Morgan, *Iolo Morganwg*, 1975, is an accessible study in English, and his volume *The Eighteenth Century Renaissance*, 1981, an excellent account of the revival of interest in Welsh antiquities. Welsh folklorists of the nineteenth century are discussed in their British context in Richard Dorson, *The British Folklorists: A History*, 1968. E. G. Bowen's, *Geography, Culture and Habitat: Selected Essays (1925–75) of E. G. Bowen*, 1976, reflects the development of his views on the human geography of Wales.

Index

133